ALSO BY DOUG HALL

WITH DAVID WECKER

———

Jump Start Your Brain

A Proven Method for
Increasing Creativity up to 500%

MAKING

THE

COURAGE

CONNECTION

Finding the Courage to Journey
from Fear to Freedom

DOUG HALL
with David Wecker

A FIRESIDE BOOK
Published by
Simon & Schuster

FIRESIDE
Rockefeller Center
1230 Avenue of the Americas
New York, NY 10020

David Wecker columns copyright © 1988–1995 by the *Cincinnati Post*.
Used by permission.

First Fireside Edition 1998

FIRESIDE and colophon are registered trademarks
of Simon & Schuster Inc.

Designed by Kate Nichols

Manufactured in the United States of America

1   3   5   7   9   10   8   6   4   2

Library of Congress Cataloging-in-Publication Data

Hall, Doug, date.
[Maverick mindset]
Making the courage connection : finding the courage to journey
from fear to freedom / Doug Hall with David Wecker.
p.   cm.
Originally published: The maverick mindset. New York : Simon &
Schuster, 1997.
1. Self-realization.   2. Courage.   3. Fear.   I. Wecker, David.
II. Title.
[BJ1470.H35   1998]
179'.6—DC21   97–38080   CIP
ISBN 0-684-82701-8
0-684-83928-8 (pbk)

Previously titled *The Maverick Mindset*.

Dedicated to Jean and Buzz Hall

Whose love, confidence, and faith
give me the courage to seek the Maverick Mindset

Thanks, Mom and Dad

The words on these pages would not have been possible
without the wisdom and inspiration of my family.
Special thanks to my high school sweetheart, my best friend,
my wife, Debbie Hall.
Extra special thanks to my children
Kristyn, Tori, and Brad for their love and support
throughout my on-the-job parenting training.

Special Thanks

Thanks, too, to these friends who encouraged and inspired: Hannah Buchanan, Jack Gordon, Sandie Glass, Mike Katz, Debbie Hall, Ellen Guidera, Tessa Westermeyer, Tod Gentille, Tracy Duckworth, Steve Klein, Lauren Avery, Adam Hansen, Sue Bamonte, Miki Reilly, Michelle Martin, Roger Greene.

Special thanks to Mary Ann Naples, our editor at Simon & Schuster, for her wisdom and inspiration.

Special thanks to those who took the time to read the raw first draft and provide their insights: Miki Reilly, Michelle Martin, Sandie Glass, Debbie Hall, Tessa Westermeyer, Hazel Hall, Pam Twist, Jim Bangel, Betty Kuhlman, Ann Badanes, Tod Gentille, Joel Miller, Peter de Jager, Bill Ernst, Karen Schenk, Steve and Mary Friedberg, Jack Bianchi, Paul Duplace, Craig Kurz, Liam Killeen.

Thanks to the *Cincinnati Post* and Paul Knue for granting permission to use material from David Wecker's newspaper columns.

Contents

Introduction

This book is about having the courage to live free from conformity and the grit to stand alone. It's about an insistence on thinking for oneself instead of following the crowd, no matter how large the crowd may be. It's about the willingness to take the riskier, rockier, less traveled path because you know it's right. It's about having the wherewithal to listen to what your heart tells you is true—and then doing it—even when your brain tells you to take the safer, more logical route.

For each of us, the journey from fear to freedom is different. For some, it's bred in at an early age by family, friends, and circumstances. For others, it arises from a middle age dissatisfaction with conformity. For others, it's a slow, steady struggle that unfolds as they successfully face one fear after another. And sadly, for many others, the process of achieving emancipation doesn't begin until retirement.

In these pages, you'll find wisdom and inspiration for discovering for the first time or rediscovering once again the highest order of courage. This book is about the gumption it takes to look for a better job, drop a bad habit or leave a relationship that's gone bad and can't be made right. It's about summoning up the courage to follow your own heart and lead a life of fulfillment.

People often are unfulfilled simply because they lack the courage to choose fulfillment. People often are unhappy in their careers, for example, but they're afraid to take the first step toward change. It's not merely that so many of us are confined to lives of quiet desperation—it's almost as if we insist on it.

Most of us live in fear. We keep our noses clean and our eyes to the ground, never looking too far beyond our next step. We mind our own business, take our orders from someone else and adapt ourselves to settle into the chain of command. When we listen to our hearts and pursue goals for which we feel real passion, we can feel that we have limitless potential. But too often, we live our lives through the expectations of others. We let our fears grow into dragons that fill us with doubts and excuses, ultimately paralyzing us.

Courage helps us create a life worth living. When you cultivate courage, you can take control over your life and the direction it takes. You lead your life instead of letting it lead you. And you tap into a sense of accomplishment, adventure, and anticipation that builds with each day.

Courage makes it possible to do the right thing when the right thing is unpopular. With courage, you can reach beyond yourself. It takes courage to turn a dream into a reality. It takes courage just to have a dream in the first place. But where can you find courage? How much is enough? And how can you use courage to draw true satisfaction from your life?

My name is Doug Hall. I spent ten years developing new products and marketing strategies for Procter & Gamble. These days, through my own company, Richard Saunders International, I advise people at some of the world's largest corporations—among them, Nike, Procter & Gamble, AT&T, Walt Disney, Compaq, Kellogg's, Hillenbrand Industries, Minnesota Power, and American Express—as to how they can find the inspiration and courage to embark on new multimillion-dollar business ventures.

These corporations are far from what you could consider everyday organizations. And the people on their payrolls have some of the best, brightest minds you'll find anywhere. But they feel every bit as much anxiety about change and risk as you felt when you knew in your heart that everyone around you was wrong—and that if you didn't stand up and tell them what was right, no one would.

I've seen corporate executives literally grow sick with fear at the prospect of having to propose and pursue a revolutionary new idea—which is, in the big picture, the only kind of idea worth having. In our Eureka! inventing projects with corporate clients, we work together from morning to night for three intense days. The result is a stripping away of political posturing and a revelation of the most human and fundamental of fears and anxieties. Week after week, I see outwardly strong men and women come face to face with fear and the need for courage.

In my own life, I've often borrowed courage from stories about the courage of others. And I've often seen others use such stories to help their own courage. In almost every case, the stories with the greatest impact are the simple ones.

In the following pages, you'll find a collection of principles for living life well. Each principle is illustrated with one or more tales of courage in real-life situations. The stories in these pages are true, to the best of my knowledge. However, in a very few instances, some identities or details have been modified as a personal courtesy.

You'll notice, too, that each chapter is prefaced with a quote from a friend or a family member about courage and gumption. These are people of all ages and from all sorts of backgrounds; people who have faced all kinds of different challenges in their lives. Gleaning their insights and sifting through their personal philosophies to find these quotes was a large part of what made the writing of this book such a rewarding experience.

From the time of my boyhood in Maine, I've ignored conventional wisdom. I've found that the more I trust in myself and do what I believe to be the right thing in the right way, the richer my life journey becomes. My life is a happy one, and it's getting better with age. I'm living my personal dream. I sleep soundly each night and awaken each morning with energy and enthusiasm because I'm doing what I really love to do.

I believe happiness is within everyone's grasp. From bricklayer to corporate chief, everyone has the ability to make his or her life more rewarding. The secret is in pushing your individual courage horizons so you can control your fear, contain your doubts, and find room to stretch, grow and lead the life you've always wanted to live.

In general, the chapters of *Making the Courage Connection* will take you, step by step, from kindling courage in the face of total fear to achieving the kind of long-range confidence we each need to be truly free. At the same time, each chapter is meant to stand on its own, so that you can open this book at any point and find something to encourage you to pursue your own path.

Should you find yourself opening *Making the Courage Connection* at this particular point, I'd like you to consider what it is that separates people who have gumption from people who don't. I believe the difference is that while some of us are working to set our life trajectories, many more are simply riding along, reacting to change instead of creating positive changes for themselves.

It may seem that the world is packed with circumstances beyond your control. It is. But that doesn't necessarily mean *you* have to spin out of control. You still have control over yourself, your state of mind, your skills, and, if you persevere, your destiny. Whether you choose to exert control is another matter altogether.

Despite the swirl of the world changing around us, our lives today have direct parallels to the early American colonists. Then as now, survival and prosperity were driven by initiative. In the 1700s, it was far easier to live the civilized life in England than to travel to the wilderness, running the risks of hard work, cold winters, and hungry bears. The choice the early Americans made was voluntary. Hope fueled their courage. And they chose to give up the lives they knew for lives they didn't know, because the unknown carried the potential for more.

Today, you have the same choice. You can stay where you are, or you can go after something more. This book will help you find courage when you feel like surrendering and falling in step with the expectations of others. Because few things are sadder than looking back on your life and saying, "I wish I had . . ."

In the end, all we really have working for us is the freedom of choice. But it takes courage to exercise that freedom and be truly free. Once and for all.

Step on the Gas,
Not the Brakes

*You have to wind yourself up to find courage.
It's easier to submit to whatever is. You have
to shake yourself and say, "No, this isn't what
I'm going to accept."*

HAZEL HALL, AGE 88

When you take action, you build momentum for courage. You can think and rethink until you overthink all the what-if's. Or you can take a step or two forward and get an entirely new perspective. When you take action, entirely new possibilities reveal themselves to you.

One Christmas, my wife gave me a certificate for three days of driving lessons at a professional racing school. The course was held at a track in Florida with specially equipped cars. It was everything the brochure promised it would be.

I remember one exercise in particular—the "lane toss," also known as the "cookie toss." The idea was to show students when to use the accelerator and when to apply the brake. I climbed behind the wheel of a BMW 325i equipped with tires that were utterly devoid of tread and drove to the far end of a quarter-mile strip of asphalt that was divided into three lanes. I was told to park in what was called the "skid lane." At the other end of the track, over each lane, was a light that flashed either green or red.

I was given the signal to gun the car toward the traffic lights. As I slammed from first to second to third gear, nearing sixty miles an hour as I approached the lights, the instructor switched two lights to red and one to green. My task was to "toss" my car to the green lane without spinning out of control.

The first attempt was closely supervised. I was told ahead of time roughly what to expect. Still, panic struck when the lights switched. I instinctively hit the brakes and yanked at the wheel, sending the car careening into a nauseating tailspin. My heart constricted as the BMW crunched a dozen traffic cones and I imagined myself slamming into cement trucks, school buses, and a pack of Cub Scouts. I could almost see the car exploding in a high-octane inferno.

I came to a stop across two lanes. My instructor walked over to the car, looked over the situation and, in a slow, studied drawl, told me he had good news and not-so-good news. The good news was that, judging by the determination with which I had hit the brakes, I had fast reflexes. The not-so-good news was, fast reflexes wouldn't help me much because, having spun out so extravagantly, I was dead. I'd hit the wrong pedal and locked the brakes. When your brakes are locked, you lose control; you can't steer unless your tires are rotating.

I tried again. This time, I kept my foot on the gas and never touched the brakes. The car responded beautifully. In exercise after exercise, the instructors showed us how to use the accelerator to avoid accidents and how, in many instances, you're asking for trouble when you stand on the brakes.

That's how it is. If you simply slam the brakes, you lose control. If you want to live, you have to use the gas, only applying the brakes intermittently.

Courage is found in action. Action happens when you have

confidence in the probability that the outcome will be successful. The key word, of course, is "probability." Nothing is ever certain. There are no sure things. Every action we attempt has a finite probability of success or failure.

Conventional wisdom teaches us that before taking action— that is, before taking a chance—you should understand everything there is to know about your subject of inquiry. In reality, life doesn't offer much opportunity to sift through mountains of information. It's true that learning, practicing, and understanding aren't to be overlooked, when the chances afford themselves. But we have to understand that, sometimes, the only way to really learn is to take action.

There's no better way to learn than by wading into the fray. It makes good, rational sense. After all, you couldn't call yourself a basketball player or a concert pianist without going out on the court or onto the stage and taking action.

Besides, courage is not a lesson you teach to someone else. Courage has to be learned—and earned. You have to initiate it in yourself. Because it's only through putting yourself at risk, by making yourself vulnerable to failure, that you can arrive at courage.

The reason we often fail to take action is also rational. We tend to overthink our options; our minds become our enemies.

Some people are actually addicted to their fears. They have the unfortunate ability to take small fears and blow them into horrific fire-breathing dragons of fear. They have doctors who prescribe tranquilizers to treat their symptoms. But they seldom dig into the root of the problem.

Taken to the extreme, fear addicts retreat into all-encompassing paranoia. They become overwhelmed with an absolute conviction that everything they do or say or think is wrong. They find conspiracies around every corner. At any minute, they expect the sky to come crashing down on their heads. They've lost all hope.

Napoleon said it: "Courage is like love; it must have hope for nourishment." What does your mind nourish? Does it nourish fear or courage, despair or hope?

A good friend of mine, Tod Gentille, suggests a simple system for gaining control over your mind in order to find the courage to take action. Tod's system focuses on removing fears from the treadmill of your imagination and translating them into concrete terms.

All it requires is a sheet of paper and a pencil. Draw three vertical columns on the sheet. On top of the first, write *Pro*; on top of the second, write *Con*; on top of the third, write *Pro*. List the pros and cons of taking action on the task ahead of you in the first two columns. In the third column, list ways to turn the con in the second column into a pro. When you're finished, your total number of pros should outnumber your cons. Essentially, you've ganged up on your fears.

Or you can label the columns *Gas*, *Brakes*, and *Gas*. Now, in very direct terms, you're dealing with reasons to move forward and reasons to hold back.

If you want to feel the response when you step on the gas, get your foot off the brakes. Relax. Think offensively instead of defensively. Look at your life. In what ways are you standing on the brakes? In what ways are you holding back your passion, your commitment?

To realize the true potential of your life journey, keep your head up and your foot on the gas. Because before you can get going, you first have to go.

Courage Connections

I believe courage is a tangible thing. It's found in the footsteps of those who have come before us, just as we'll leave some for those who follow after us.

KARI McCAMPBELL, AGE 22

Imagine you're a child watching a scary movie, and the monster is your worst fear personified. Suddenly, the monster fills the screen. You reach instinctively for your best friend in the next seat. You grab your best friend's hand and hold on for dear life. In that simple act, you're fortified. You feel less afraid.

You've just made the most basic form of courage connection. You've borrowed courage from your best friend and, in this case, from the fact that you're not alone.

Making a courage connection is a way to boost your gumption when you're facing fear. It happens when you establish a link between yourself and a person, a place, a time, or an experience from your past—or to a figure or event in history from which you can draw inspiration.

Courage connections come in handy when you're facing down a fear; they can give you that extra ounce of *oomph* you need to keep going when everyone around you is falling apart. Since fear exists primarily in your mind, it follows that you can use your mind as a weapon to fight it. Courage connections can enable you to sublimate fear. By filling your mind with the hope, vision, and inspiration you get when you plug into a courage connection, you leave less room in your mind for insecurity and doubt. This concept was revealed to me when my father and I took my children snorkeling in New London Bay off Prince Edward Island.

From the deck of our boat, the ocean waves looked mild. From the water, even a few inches of swell can set your heart to pounding. I went in first, but I wasn't sure if the kids would follow. Seeing as how they were only four, six, and eight years old, I wasn't about to put any pressure on them.

We decided to let them try it one at a time, using a six-foot length of rope Dad found below deck as a safety line. One end was tied to my wrist; the other, to the wrist of the junior snorkeler. To my surprise, each of my children wanted to take a turn. But I noticed that whenever the rope became slack, I'd feel a sharp tug. Whenever they couldn't feel me pulling on my end, they'd pull on their end to make sure I was still there.

My children showed internal courage when they jumped over the side of the boat. But they also had an external source of courage—the rope. It was their guarantee that, should a problem occur, their dad could reel them in. It was as if courage was pumped from me to them through the rope. All three kids gave voice to this, one a time as they joined me in the water. Their signal to put our heads underwater to see what was down there was, "Ready, Dad? Okay, let's do it!" The operative word was "let's"— as in "not just me" or "not just you." It was the both of us, or it was nothing. Their strength in that situation came from their faith and confidence in me.

You can use your mind to make the same sort of courage connections my children did with the safety line. Courage connections take many forms:

- A courage connection can be made with a training program you've completed. The sheer repetitive nature of training engenders confidence, which in turn gives rise to courage. If, for example, you're in the home stretch of a marathon and you're connecting mentally to all the flights of stairs, the sprints, and the kilometers of hills you've conquered in the process of training, you reinforce yourself to cover the distance between you and the finish line.

- A courage connection can be made with a parallel experience when you overcame even greater adversity than your current situation. For instance, if you once found courage to stop smoking, you can use that experience as a source of courage to drop another bad habit. In my creative endeavors, my personal experiential touchstone is a trip I made to Capitol Hill to invent ideas for balancing the federal budget. Having looked into the beady eyes of the Washington bureaucracy, I can't imagine ever fearing another creative challenge again.

- A courage connection can be made with a mentor who inspired you, who gave principle and purpose to your actions. I've found this kind of inspiration from many people. In difficult times, I recall their memory and their counsel. Faced with manufacturing or engineering issues, I often connect with my father and the many lessons he taught me. When evaluating marketing ideas, I often connect with Ross Love of Procter & Gamble, who taught me how to think big. When evaluating a marketing strategy, I often connect with Mark Upson of Procter & Gamble, who taught me the importance of focus.

- A courage connection can be with figures from history. In

my case, the model is Benjamin Franklin. His wisdom, wit, and ability to succeed in a wide array of endeavors have been a bountiful source of inspiration, both in my personal life and in my career. I've taken the Benjamin Franklin approach with my own business, relying on outside alliances instead of hiring a large internal staff, leveraging licensing as a profit tool and emphasizing the written word.

• A courage connection can even be made with a piece of music. When I interviewed for my first job out of college, I was scared half out of my mind. As I entered the doors, my pockets filled with magic tricks from my career as Merwyn the Magician, I hummed the theme from the original "Rocky" for inspiration—you know, the tune from the scene where Rocky is running up the steps of the Philadelphia Art Museum. *Da da da—da da daaaaaah.*

Sometimes it's better not to make one huge, all-encompassing courage connection when you're facing a fearful situation. Sometimes, it's better to make a series of smaller ones because, when you add them all together, they become a far more formidable force.

Such was the case when my friend and coauthor, David Wecker, harvested the honey from a pair of beehives in the field next to his house. He connected with a protective bee suit, a device known to beekeepers as a smoker and Margaret and Ray Lauer, a couple in their mid-60s who actually knew something about honeybees.

Having spent the summer tracking the comings and goings of his bees through high-powered binoculars, David decided it finally was time to harvest the honey. He'd put it off as long as he could. But over the previous few weeks, it had become necessary to inspect the hives personally, so he'd know if there was any honey to get, since getting honey is the whole point of beekeeping.

This was a step he was reluctant to take. His understanding of bees was limited to the knowledge that, basically, bees do only two things—make honey and sting people. That last part is the part you have to watch out for. You could be the nicest person in the world, and bees would still try to sting you if you were stealing their honey.

David's first and primary source of courage was his bee suit. You sweat a lot in a bee suit, but you'd sweat more if you weren't wearing one. A bee suit is roughly comparable to the sort of outfit Chem-Dyne workers wear to clean up toxic spills—heavy coveralls that zip to the throat, canvas gloves that pull over your elbows, thick boots you can tuck your pants legs into and a pith helmet with a wire-mesh veil to protect your face while reducing your vision to that of a fruit bat. The veil zips to the collar of your coveralls. The only gap in these zippers is at Adam's apple level. You just have to hope the bees won't find it, fly inside your veil, and sting your face.

David further fortified his courage with a smoker—a handheld tin box with bellows attached. You put dead leaves, straw, and whatever tinder you can find inside the tin box, light it, close the lid and squeeze the bellows until thick, white smoke rolls out the spout. Smoke gives bees a buzz. A few squeezes of the bellows, and most bees will be too dizzy to care that you're stealing their honey. Ideally, your smoker will remain lit throughout the harvesting process. The effectiveness of your courage connection with your smoker at this point is directly related to how long it continues to generate smoke.

At this point, you're ready to lift the lid from the hive and start digging into the frames. This is where the bees store their honey. But by this time, the bees are coming at you like angry metal sparks flying off a grindstone.

If you surrender to your impulse to start swatting at the bees as they buzz around the gap in the zippers at your throat, they'll sense your fear and move in for the kill. The best thing to do is whistle a happy tune—David recommends "Three Blind Mice"— and go about your business with an air of disinterested nonchalance.

The Lauers were David's most powerful courage connection as he approached his hives for the first time. He describes Margaret and Ray as the apiary patron saints of Alexandria, Kentucky.

On the day of the harvest, the Lauers arrived at the Wecker compound in their Beemobile, an old Ford pickup they use to tend the seventy-five or so hives they have scattered around Campbell County. Ray and Margaret don't own bee suits. The only protective gear they use is veils and a smoker. Their level of experience and expertise gave them far more courage than their rookie counterpart felt.

Ray explained to David that the trick is to separate the bees from their honey. Honey is no good to you if you don't. You can smoke out most bees. But you have to stink out the stubborn ones with a "fume board," which is soaked with a liquid that smells like it was collected from a cat with a kidney disorder.

After a few minutes of fuming, the bees retreated deeper into the hive. As Margaret lifted out frames heavy with amber honey, worker bees crawled all over her bare arms and hands. She brushed them away gently with a soft-bristled brush, taking pains not to hurt a single one.

"Go home, girls," she told them. They did, too.

David thinks Margaret may be the bravest woman he has ever known. He felt a lot better about digging into his beehives with her and her husband there. The smoker and the bee suit helped, too. Between his helpers and his gear, he'd connected to all the courage he needed.

To find your courage connections, stop reading for a moment and reflect on your personal history. Think of the people who have inspired you over the years. Think of all the biographies and life stories you've read or heard. What were their sources of courage? Think of times when you faced fear head-on and won. Think of the lessons you've learned and the experiences you've had over the years where the mere memory of them fills you with strength.

Commit your list of strength sources to paper. Put a copy in your wallet or purse, in your car, or on your bathroom mirror. If you have a written list when fear strikes—and it will, if you're truly alive—you'll have a touchstone to reinforce your courage.

Don't listen to the small voice inside that accuses you of showing a frail spirit when you make a courage connection. You're simply admitting there's someone or something larger than you from which you can draw strength. As Benjamin Franklin said, "We must all hang together or most assuredly we will all hang separately."

Believe to Achieve

It takes courage to change, to like ourselves, to trust when people in our lives have not been trustworthy: to love, and be loved.

NANCI HARTLAND, AGE 52

You've got to have faith. If you don't believe in yourself, no one else will.

I'm very liberal in terms of what constitutes a proper expression of faith. My forefathers came to America because they were persecuted in England for expressing religious views apart from those held by the king. My great (nine times) grandfather, John Lathrop, though ordained a deacon of the Church of England in 1607, was exiled for failing to adhere to the "proper religious views." Other branches of the Hall family tree were persecuted for being Quakers.

I choose to attend Saint Timothy's Episcopal Church, in no small part because I find inspiration and wisdom from the ministers, Roger and Nancy Greene. But I find no fault in any other organized or unorganized source of faith. Freedom of religion is not to be taken lightly.

More important than what flavor of church you attend is your faith in a fundamental spiritual force. From faith comes a reflective strength in your personal state of being. From faith comes a sense of destiny and purpose.

Courage connections are, in effect, about faith—faith in others, in ourselves, in our individual missions and in the rightness of our hearts. Faith can be focused on God, but it also can be focused on people. In almost every case, the latter is more difficult to have than the former because, more often than not, people will let you down. We've all had experiences when we thought someone was looking out for us, only to discover they weren't.

The other day, my friend Mike Katz invited me to an indoor rock-climbing facility. The place had a forty-foot simulated rock wall studded with nubs not much bigger than goose eggs. The idea is, you grab onto this nub and put your foot on that nub. And somehow, you make a vertical ascent.

I climbed into a rope harness, and immediately experienced intense fear. Mike held the safety line and up I went—one foot, two feet, three feet, until I was looking down on the rest of the world from an altitude of ten feet. Mike looked like an ant. My heart was pounding like a jackhammer. "Okay, okay," I hollered. "I think I've got the idea. You can go ahead and let me down now."

Mike didn't think so. He told me I should practice falling. He said the only way I'd learn to have any faith in my support system was to fall a few times in order to feel it catching me. He ordered me to climb another ten feet. When I was ready, he told me to lay back, let go, and fall away from the wall. He assured me that, logically and rationally, I had nothing to fear—he had a firm grip on the safety line, the whole thing was properly strung through the belay pressure clip and the line could hold three of me. He further explained that hundreds of thousands of people had done what I was about to do and that they'd lived to ripe old ages.

Logically and rationally, I was convinced. I took a deep breath and let go.

In a split second, as I fell from a dizzying height of nearly twenty feet, I went from feeling logically and rationally convinced to as close to a total, blind, apoplectic panic as I've ever been and ever hope to be. It seemed as if I'd fallen seven or eight feet before the line caught me. When I opened my eyes, I saw that it was more like five inches.

That wasn't so bad. So I tried again. And again. Each time, my faith in my support system grew. And as my faith grew, I had the confidence to climb higher and higher.

So it is with life. When you're facing a fear for the first time, having faith is sometimes the key to gaining confidence. Only by falling and building faith in the strength of your support system can you build real confidence.

Having faith in people is a vital part of being a member of the human race. None of us can go it alone. We all need help.

One way to find faith in others and in ourselves is to make a courage connection with whatever you wish to call the supreme being. As for me, I find great strength in God.

It was a connection I made in my early teens, when my grandmother loaned me a copy of Norman Vincent Peale's *The Power of Positive Thinking,* a book that translates faith and religion into something you can use every day. I read and reread that book— and strongly recommend it to anyone who wants to live life to the fullest.

Peale wrote of enlisting God as an ally in your life journey. It's advice I've held firm to all my life. Peale encourages his readers to use the Bible as a source of extraordinary strength. If you're running low on courage, look up these passages and think about what they have to say:

- Philippians 4:4–13
- Psalms 23:1–6
- Deuteronomy 31:7–8
- Psalms 27:1–14
- 2 Chronicles 32:7–8
- Romans 8:31

I haven't reprinted the verses because I believe that, with a little wandering through the Bible, you might find a more powerfully inspirational passage of your own.

Peale's book and the teachings of my early family life nurtured within me a personal relationship with God that has given me great faith in the face of overwhelming fear. When I'm being tested, it helps me to chat with God in everyday language, to enlist His support and express my fears, my faith, my thanks for all the blessings in my life. I speak with God in an open, honest manner about what is in my heart and on my mind. I've never heard God's voice reply in an audible way, but I've felt a sense of peace and calm that's truly awesome in its power. When you can call on your faith, you know you're not alone in your challenge. You know the Lord is with you and that, even in the darkest times, He hears you.

The story of Bonnie Darwish illustrates how you can call on your faith to help you through dark times. One night, Bonnie and her husband, Jeff, were driving north toward Cincinnati in their LeBaron. They didn't see the eighteen-wheeler coming off the eastbound ramp until it was too late. Bonnie's right ankle was pulverized in the accident; pieces of bone were lost at the scene. Her right foot was black by the time the ambulance arrived at St. Luke Hospital. The doctors didn't know if they could save it.

As the paramedics carried her off the ambulance and wheeled

her into the emergency room, two nurses recalled that Bonnie was engaged in a conversation with someone they took to be God. Somehow, they said, she was calm. Vascular specialist Dr. Kevin Martin decided that, if there was to be any hope of saving Bonnie's leg, a collapsed artery in her right leg would have to be replaced immediately with a section of vein from her left leg.

"That night, my family came into ICU and prayed that the blood would flow and my leg would be saved," Bonnie says. "It wasn't but five minutes later, and the toes on my right foot were pink again. Pinker than the toes on my left foot. The nurses couldn't believe it."

Since then, Bonnie has surprised a lot of people—Dr. Martin, for one: "She definitely has had an unusual, remarkable recovery. We attribute it to the fact that she's relatively young and in excellent physical condition." But he said her ankle will never be normal. "My goal is to get it to the point where she can get around on it again," he said. "Then again, with the recovery she's had so far, she may exceed our expectations."

That was Bonnie's plan. Anything is possible with God, she figured. And indeed, she did exceed her doctors' expectations. Each day, at the time of this writing, she walks a mile. Each week, she puts in a minimum of thirty miles on her bicycle.

Five months after the accident, Bonnie showed up for her regular Thursday night exercise class in the basement of the First Assembly of God Church in Alexandria, Kentucky. The toes of her right foot poked from a cast that rode up her shin to just below her knee. She needed help getting through the door, what with the wheelchair and all. But not much help. Every day, Bonnie needed less and less help.

When the instructor slid a tape into the player, punched a button and turned up the volume, Bonnie hauled herself up on a walker and pumped her legs. She worked her arms. She kicked higher than anyone in the class. Bonnie had faith. For a forty-eight-year-old grandmother who had her right leg all but torn off in a car crash five months before, Bonnie looked good.

Bonnie's physicians had one set of expectations about her recovery. Bonnie had other expectations. While her doctors worked merely to save her leg, believing that was the most they could reasonably expect to accomplish, Bonnie set her mind on something more. Instead of listening to her doctors, she tuned her mind to a higher authority. Instead of giving in to fear and despair, she nourished her courage with hope and faith. And her body followed her mind.

If you wish to overcome your fears and find the courage to be who you really are, you have to believe you're worthy of achieving your goals. If you don't believe in yourself, you have no chance of success.

Let's take a quick inventory of all the reasons why you're worth believing in.

Do you try in your day-to-day actions to be honest?

Do you try in your day-to-day actions to be trustworthy?

Do you try in your day-to-day actions to be loyal?

Do you try in your day-to-day actions to be kind?

Do you try in your day-to-day actions to be friendly?

Do you try in your day-to-day actions to be dependable?

Do you try in your day-to-day actions to be fair?

Do you try in your day-to-day actions to be respectful?

Do you try in your day-to-day actions to show concern for others' feelings?

Do you try in your day-to-day actions to do the right things in the right way?

I'll bet you answered yes to far more of those questions than not. People are fundamentally good. We prefer to do the right thing. But because of the pressures of everyday living, we sometimes lose sight of our basic values. Deep down, you're a great person. Once you believe as much in your heart of hearts, your courage to be you can grow a thousandfold.

Define Your Mission

*Courage is coaching Little League Baseball and
pinch-hitting for your best hitter with your weakest
hitter in the final inning of a tied game because you
promised everyone would get to bat in every game. It's
easy to change your mind—it takes courage to honor
your promises.*

MIKE KATZ, AGE 37

Before you can bask in the warm glow of accomplishment,
before you can begin to build momentum for your courage,
you must have a clear sense of a mission.

Courage that endures from day to day and year to year feeds
on two factors—one, having a sense of mission, and two, believing
in your heart that the task you face is one that matters. To have
courage that endures, you must have a quest. But more than that,
you must feel a personal calling for that quest. The quest can be
outwardly directed, as in making the world a better place, or introspective, as in summoning the inner strength to change some
aspect of yourself that you want to change.

In either case, having a goal helps you persevere through failures. And you will experience failures, because the only way to
avoid failures is to do nothing. On the other hand, the best way to
do something is to have a goal. And the more relevant and important your mission is, the braver and more persistent you'll be.

My daughter, Kristyn, learned to stand in this manner. As our firstborn, this bundle of joy was expected to learn how to do everything at once: stand, run, juggle, recite the Gettysburg Address, tell complicated jokes with perfect timing, discover a cure for cancer, and so on. These, after all, are the perfectly reasonable expectations all first-time parents have of their offspring.

One day, I was trying to get Kristyn to stand at my sister Pam's house in Waterville, Maine. My method was to lift her to a standing position, gently withdraw my support, then lean back with paternal pride as my daughter performed her first *plié*. My method wasn't working; each time I lifted Kristyn to a standing position, her knees buckled and she slumped like a small, unmotivated sack of potatoes back into a sitting position. She was suffering from a complete lack of inspiration.

Enter Garcia, my sister's tomcat. He hopped onto the counter above her. Suddenly, Kristyn had found inspiration. Or it had found her. What was that furry thing? In an instant, without thinking, she was standing.

She had wordlessly declared her mission—to reach out and touch Garcia. Her desire had overwhelmed any potential fear. Having her mission in mind, it never occurred to her that she would have to do something she'd never done before to achieve it.

Seek out ways to give meaning to your life journey. Many times, you'll find you have a mission, but you haven't given it due credit. Perhaps you haven't recognized the larger goodness that will result from completing your mission. I believe we're all driven by an inner sense of rightness. The challenge is to bring forth the element of rightness in your mission and recognize it for what it is. In articulating the fundamental good that will come about as a result of your mission, your resolve will be strengthened. And you will realize a higher purpose to your goal.

Think about the fears lying in wait to ambush you. Why are you considering pursuing a specific goal? What are the obstacles? What's in it for you—or your family, your company, your community, the world?

When you examine your mission in the bright light of day, many of your fears turn out to be toothless vampires that crumble into piles of dust. Let them go—they aren't worth keeping. Other times, the mere act of talking out loud about your mission will give you the courage and confidence you need to get started.

One summer day, a guy I'd never seen before stopped by the office looking for advice. He introduced himself as Ed and described himself as an overworked, underpaid accountant. He had a dream for a new kind of delivery service. His eyes grew wide as he described it to me.

It was clear that he was deeply in love with his dream. I wondered why he didn't quit the accounting firm and give it a shot. His reason was, he was scared. He'd never kicked anything off before. He'd never been in the forefront of anything. So I asked him, what was the worst that could happen? He said that, as an accountant, he'd seen lots of small businesses go belly-up. And he figured the worst that could happen was that he could go broke.

Of course. Bankruptcy was a distinct possibility. But he seemed in good health, and he appeared to have many working years ahead of him. I asked if he'd prefer to continue in his present position or endure the humiliation of declaring bankruptcy not once but twice—if in his third venture, he knew he would succeed, if he'd have a business that would provide his family with a comfortable living. Maybe he wouldn't be rich, but he'd be his own boss.

Ed the overworked, underpaid accountant thought that

wouldn't be too bad if, in the end, he'd turned his dream into a reality. Yes, he would endure the humiliation and discomfort of going bankrupt twice if, on his third attempt, he would succeed,
even if only to a modest degree.

At that point, his decision was a simple matter of mathemat-
ics. While it's entirely possible for a new venture to fail, the odds
of going bankrupt three times are exceedingly low. In fact, I told
him, if he put his heart and soul into a business mission, if he
learned from his mistakes, if he was willing to keep his eye on his
mission through two failures, he was virtually guaranteed to be
successful.

A year later, I heard Ed had resigned his accounting job and
launched a new kind of delivery service. And he hadn't gone bankrupt. Not even once.

All sorts of things can inspire a sense of mission—an obligation, a
childhood dream, an act of kindness, a sense of duty, an urgent di-
rective from your editor on deadline, a sudden need in your family. Once you've heard the call and your mission is in place, you're
better equipped to handle the contingencies that crop up in your
path. Granted, you may run the risk of being called eccentric, depending on the nature of your mission. Don't let that stop you.
People thought Einstein, Franklin, Gandhi, and Edison were eccentric, too. Besides, it's far better to take a position than never
believe in anything.

That's how it was for Alvin Straight of Laurens, Iowa. It could
be argued that Alvin was a bit on the eccentric side. But his cause
was righteous. His is a story of a clearly focused mission, inspired
by his caring for his brother.

In the summer of his seventy-third year, Alvin embarked on a
mission after learning his brother had had a stroke. Alvin decided

to visit his brother, whose name was Henry. The problem was, how to get there. Henry lived 425 miles away in Wisconsin. And since Alvin's eyesight wasn't nearly as good as it once was, he no longer had a driver's license.

What he needed was a conveyance he could operate without a license. He settled on a 1966 John Deere lawn tractor with an eight-horsepower engine, since there was no law saying a person needed a license to operate a lawnmower. He stashed a supply of clothing, food, camping gear, and the proceeds from two Social Security checks in a wooden box, then lashed the box to a small trailer. And one July day in 1994, he headed off for the far side of Wisconsin.

It was slow going but Alvin had a clear mission. He drove on the shoulder, where there was one. He broke down a half dozen times. On a good ten-hour day, he'd put fifty miles behind him. And on the fifteenth of August, only a couple miles from Henry's place, the drive belt gave out. Fortunately, a farmer on a full-scale tractor happened along and gave Alvin a tow the rest of the way.

On arriving at Henry's, Alvin was gratified to find that his brother wasn't feeling too badly. In fact, Henry came outside when Alvin pulled up and helped him unhitch his trailer. Alvin stayed with his brother for a month, long enough to make sure he was well on the way to a full recovery. And then, while there was still something left of the warm weather, he climbed back on his John Deere lawn tractor and drove it back to Iowa.

By that time, Alvin had the hang of it. His mission was to see his brother, and he knew his mission as well as he knew the back of his tractor seat. Each time his tractor broke down, he learned something. All the national news wires picked up the story and made him out to be a hero. But the way he looked at it, he was a common man with a purpose—and that alone gave him the determination to see it through.

Some missions occupy entire lifetimes. Walter Koch took up such a mission, one that grew out of a dream halfway around the world and shaped his entire life. Walter was orphaned at the age of seven and became a ward of the Campbell County Children's Home in Newport, Kentucky. Most of what he learned, he taught himself. He stayed at the children's home until he was sixteen, when he struck out on his own to become a carpenter. But he never forgot the children's home. He often thought about how it should have been to grow up there, how it could be if he were in charge.

When World War II broke out a year later, he joined the Seabees. One October night in 1942, when he was with the Seabees in Guadalcanal, Walter had a dream about the Campbell County Children's Home. It was filled with happy children, and they all called him Dad. Years later, he would describe the dream as the defining moment in his life's mission.

He returned home in 1944. Two years later, he was offered the superintendent's job at the children's home. He accepted on the condition the home would be remodeled or rebuilt elsewhere. After all, the old home had been around since 1884. The Protestant Ladies Auxiliary, which ran the home, agreed. In 1947, they purchased a twenty-five-acre tract of rolling farmland. Three years later, ground was broken for a new children's home. Walter, his wife, Zella, and the children worked together, like a big family. The boys poured footers, put in sidewalks and did much of the carpentry; the girls held bake sales to raise money. Largely because of their efforts, the home was soon debt-free.

Walter never had any children of his own. But more than 300

children called him Dad. They're all grown now. Walter himself is 87, but he still remembers all their names. "I loved those children—every one of them," he said.

Each year, for as long as he lives, any number of his children will extend invitations to Walter to share Christmas with them. Or Thanksgiving or Easter or a wedding or a graduation or a birthday. For as long as Walter lives, his children will respond to a commitment that began with a dream half a century ago.

Having a strong set of values makes it easier to assign a sense of mission to whatever goal you pursue. When your life is grounded in the values of family, friends and faith—when you have the deep conviction that you know the difference between what's true and what's false, what's right and what's wrong—you're far more likely to keep a clear focus on your destination, whatever it might be.

On Your Mark, Get Set, Take a First Step

Courage is looking fear right in the eye and saying, "Get the hell out of my way, I've got things to do."

CRAIG KURZ, AGE 34

When you're trying to break free of fear, the first step is the most difficult.

Steve Roller knows how hard it can be to take that first step. He knows better than most that momentum is built one step at a time. He knows, too, that once you've taken that first step, once you've actually made the transition from thinking about a thing to trying it, you're on your way.

Steve is the leg man at Prosthetics and Orthotics of Cincinnati. His formal title is prosthetic technician, which means he builds artificial legs to replace real ones. He got into the business because he was having trouble with his own leg.

The summer before his senior year in high school, he was in an accident. A car ran a stop sign. Steve was hit broadside and thrown over his motorcycle. His right leg had to be amputated at the knee. He was what he calls "a tough fit" for a prosthetic leg.

"I spent a lot of time over the next three years going to different places, looking for a leg that felt right," Steve says. "It was a difficult time. You wonder whether you're going to be in and out of the hospital every week for the rest of your life. You wonder if you'll ever be able to get along like other people.

"I wasn't really going anywhere career-wise. Just floating, really. And my dad suggested that prosthetics might be an interesting field to get into. Turned out he was right: You get a good feeling watching a patient walk out of here with the finished product. Because if you do it right, you can't tell they aren't walking on their own legs."

Steve includes himself among his satisfied customers. He has what is known as a "Carbon Copy II" foot that puts spring in his step. And he's getting ready to switch to a new ankle that flexes, making it easier to navigate the hills. "I guess the leg of my dreams would have a Monroe Gas-Matic shock absorber and a swivel at the ankle," Steve says. But he gets along pretty well as it is. He plays basketball, volleyball, golf, and bowls in a league. Once you shuck the feeling of being handicapped, he says, you have it made.

"The hardest thing was learning to run again," he says. "I couldn't figure out why I wasn't able to. Then it dawned on me that I hadn't tried. And I just started running. All you need are two good legs."

Once Steve stopped thinking and started trying, he succeeded. It happens all the time. We get so caught up in thinking, and trying to discern reasons for why we haven't made it happen, we forget to try. When you try, you begin to build momentum. And once you're rolling along under the force of your own momentum, you'll see things that those who are stuck in their thinking modes can never even imagine. But you can't begin to generate momentum until you've taken that first step, then the next, then the one after that. Isaac Newton put it this way: "A body at rest stays at rest until a force acts on it."

You have to be that force. Don't make the mistake of thinking the safe way is to do nothing. In today's world, if you're not moving forward, the competition will leave you in the dust. Standing still is not an acceptable option. The choice could hardly be simpler: Grow or die. You can't afford to maintain the status quo, not unless you relish the thought of one day looking back on a life strewn with regrets.

Sometimes, the first step seems impossible. Your fear can be a great boulder that can't be budged. No matter how hard you push, it rolls back to where you started. It's like trying to carry a mattress up five flights of stairs. The mattress isn't all that heavy, but it's awkward. No matter where you grab it, it folds and twists and turns back on you like a living thing.

But in order to attack a fear, you have to take that first step. Here's a secret: It usually doesn't matter how you take action on your fear, as long as you take some action. Like a deer on the highway caught in the headlights of an oncoming eighteen-wheeler, you can freeze in your tracks or you can move. If you freeze, you're roadkill. If you move, in whatever direction, you increase the odds of living long enough to be caught in the headlights of another oncoming eighteen-wheeler on another day.

That's how it is with fear. If you take action, generally any action, you increase your chances of slaying the fear dragon.

Courage has a tangible quality. You can't touch it, but you can feel it. It feels like positive acceleration. Courage sends a rush of energy through your body. It makes you wake up in the morning with a feeling of wanting to wrap your hands around the day. When you take that first step, you'll feel courage. Your whole body will come alive with a vitality and an eagerness for life.

Likewise, inaction is more than just mental. When you're gripped in fear, your mouth is dry, your hands tremble. If you laugh, it's a nervous laugh. Continued paralysis generated by fear can result in serious medical conditions—depression, fatigue, insomnia, indigestion, nausea, ulcers, migraines, and all varieties of heebie-jeebies.

You're equipped with a fantastic system dealing with reactions to spontaneous situations. It's called the biological fight-or-flight response. Your pupils dilate, your sense of smell is heightened, your adrenalin kicks in, your heart pumps faster to send more blood to your muscles, and your rate of respiration increases to heighten your alertness and strength.

If you're facing a wounded water buffalo, these naturally induced responses can be important to your continued survival. In today's world, your body goes through the same responses when you're presented with frightening situations, even if you're only asking the boss for a day off. At its most basic level, courage arises from a threat to our survival as we know it.

A little fear can create an adrenaline rush that can itself be a powerful motivator. If your response to fear is to take action, you're suddenly in a position to take full advantage of these natural responses. If you freeze, you die.

Biological reactions can give you the energy to face unexpected crises. But in our everyday lives, we're more often faced with situations that build gradually, giving us time to anticipate—contingencies that are elective, selective, and require planning. We have time to get scared. So the methods for dealing with these circumstances are different.

To plan for future events that you know will fill you with fear, work on your opening lines, your first few steps, the process of gracefully dropping to one knee to ask your true love's hand in marriage. The first sixty seconds are critically important in any act of courage. In the first few moments, you establish your momentum. Positive or negative.

Think about the times you've been called on to deliver a speech, make a presentation or, in one capacity or another, perform in front of an audience. If the first few moments go smoothly, you quickly settle into a rhythm and off you go. If instead you stumble, you drop your notes and the audience laughs when you didn't think you were saying anything especially funny, you learn how it feels to twist in the wind. Your momentum sputters, and fear threatens to take control. *Tsk.* And to think you could have prepared your opening ahead of time.

Practice and preparation nurture courage. When you practice, focus your efforts first and foremost on your opening. Be absolutely certain of your first few words. Carefully plan and rehearse your first few steps until they become second nature. Think about how they might affect the conversation or the flow of events.

Whenever you begin anything, you've taken the initiative. You've given the world something to react to, instead of reacting to the world. The first steps you take from the starting block in a foot race, the first moves in a game of chess, the first incision in a surgical procedure, the first sentences in a pitch for a raise establish your tone, your pace, and your future options. And the degree to which your first few moves are successful—and the extent to which you can begin to build momentum—can be sharply enhanced through practice.

Let's say you're a concert musician suffering from a severe case of the willies. You want to project an image that reflects your music and sets the proper mood for how your audience will respond to your performance. If you walk slowly from the wings in a tuxedo and sit down at a piano decked out with a candelabra, your audience will be predisposed to settle back into their seats and take in a sedate sonata or a reflective concerto. If, on the other hand, you bound onstage in a fluorescent spandex bodysuit and start hammering away on the piano with your elbows, your audience is more likely to get up on its feet, put its hands together and put itself in a mood for some high-voltage rock 'n' roll. In either case, you've developed momentum before you've played a single note. And having developed momentum, you'll be on your way to success. The key is to get off to a strong start. Once you've put your opening behind you, the steps that follow tend to fall into place.

People often tell me they have an idea or a vision, but they don't know where to start. I ask them what they've tried and what dead ends they've encountered. Almost invariably, the answer is zero, zilch, nada. I look at them with wonder. Columbus never would have discovered America if he'd sat in Spain and just thought. By taking action, you discover, learn, and gain control over your fears.

Think about the baby who is just learning to walk. Does that baby sit in her diaper and ponder the wonders of personal locomotion—or does she pull herself up onto her feet and take that first step? What happens? She falls down. What does she do then? She gets up and tries again. And again. And again. And eventually, she gets the hang of it.

It takes that same childlike faith to conquer fear. Just take a step. Any step. You may fall down—but so what? If you wait until you can take a step without any chance of failure, you'll probably sit in your diaper a long, long time—maybe your whole life. But when you take a step, you find new courage. Trying something new is like peering over the next ridge of mountains. You gain new insights, which you can wield like a weapon against fear.

Life is an actual state of being. It's not a dream. And it happens one step at a time.

Reading, Talking, and Trying

Courage is the greatest sport there is! To score big, you have to step way outside your personal comfort zone and face your own fears head-on without a safety net.

JEFFREY STAMP, AGE 35

One of the greatest of all barriers to courage is, by its nature, especially difficult to corner. It's the fear of the unknown—as in, "I've never done anything like this before," "No telling what will happen if I do," or "I don't have all the facts." Many of us lack the courage to embark on new ventures because we insist on knowing where we're going. We want detailed itineraries with clearly focused beginnings, middles, and destinations.

Life doesn't work that way. Consider America's westward migration. The trail to California wasn't lined with Ramadas and HoJos. The pioneers in their Conestogas had to deal with contingencies along the way—rattlesnakes, brutal winters, boiling summers, broken axles, and the Rocky Mountains. Considering the odds against them, they never should have made it to L.A.

The thing about the unknown is that we don't know much about it. The point is, you can live your whole life in fear of the unknown. Or you can wade into the unknown and approach the experience as a great adventure. Don't worry too much about not knowing ahead of time how it's all going to turn out; it wouldn't be much of an adventure if somehow you could remove the element of surprise. And don't be afraid to experience something for the first time. Ralph Waldo Emerson said it: "A great part of courage is the courage of having done the thing before."

So, too, it is with life. We're more comfortable the second time than we were the first time, less awkward the third time than we were the second. On the other hand, there can't be a second or a third time until there has been a first time. That's where the unknown is. That's where you have the best opportunity to pull a sense of adventure from the unknown.

When you're approaching the unknown with a sense of adventure, some kind of fear will be a constant. In fact, fear is necessary for survival; it makes us consider in advance the consequences of our actions and keeps us from taking foolish risks. Even when you exercise courage on a regular basis, even when you "get brave," fear will never leave you. What will happen instead is that *your fear frontier will expand*; that is, you'll be able to beat back larger, more amorphous fears. As your courage grows, the boundaries of your fear frontier are pushed outward, increasing your adventure comfort zone, which in turn increases the amount of pleasure you get from life. Courage gives you the power to make choices you want to make.

Sometimes, you can conquer the unknown simply through learning, thus making the unknown known. Instead of wasting time worrying about an unknown commodity, you can spend it gathering information in order to turn the unknown inside out. Usually, the most efficient way to learn about something is to ask the right questions about it. Good interviewers are skilled at pulling information from sources who are either defensive or reluctant. Watch a good TV news interviewer and pay more attention to the questions than the answers. Consider how the questions are phrased, shaded, loaded, aimed, and fired. Notice how the responses sometimes reveal more than was intended. Look at how the interviewer fills in the blanks with follow-up questions. And when you're seeking answers to questions, consider your sources. What will put them off? What is more likely to draw them out?

But it's not enough to ask the right questions. It's also important to listen closely to the answers—or more specifically, to the emotions roiling under the surface.

When a client corporation hires me to do a job, I visit the company and talk with all the key people, one at a time. In my work, the "facts and data" aspects of a business problem usually are obvious: The client is in big trouble. What isn't known, most of the time, is how the people working on solving the problem feel about their situation. Have they given up hope? Do they acknowledge a problem exists? Is there still a spark of energy that might yet be fanned into a bonfire of revolutionary change?

Data can be quantitative, directional, or a simple function of gut instinct. I've found instinct to be as effective as hard data in shaking off the mystery of the unknown, although both have value. Think of a challenge that lies before you. Think about what you do know and what you don't know about it. My guess is, you know more than you think, but you haven't been listening closely to yourself. Few of us do. It's part of the human condition; we tend not to be very good listeners.

Instead, try committing your problem to paper. Make a list of the things you know, differentiating between what you know to be a fact and what you know to be a hunch or an instinctive reaction.

Take it a step further. Attach a percentage to each fact, hunch, or instinctive reaction indicating the probability that each piece of knowledge you've listed is actually true. Which of these un-known elements have the greatest potential impact on your situ-ation? If you wait a month to make a decision, will you know significantly more than you know today? If not, it's probably time to move forward.

Identifying your fears in writing will make it easier for you to sift truth from mere perception. It will allow you to capture what's flying around your head and balance your perspective. When we sit, we stew. The line between truth and fiction blurs. We minimize positives and amplify negatives. On paper, you can keep perceptions from inbreeding with facts.

Let's say you and your spouse have 2.2 children to support and a hefty house payment. One of you wants to go back to school. The question is, can you afford it? Stop talking, start figuring. Re-view your checkbook over the past several months and make a chart of all your expenses. Separate the necessary expenses from the optional. Compare your expenses with the working spouse's income, along with any part-time income available to the student spouse. Now you have the information you need to make a ratio-nal decision.

I have a system for turning the unknown into the known. It's a practical plan for gaining actionable knowledge. It's called *Reading, Talking, and Trying.* I've used it to learn about all kinds of subjects that were completely unknown to me, among them, photography, scuba diving, boating, deep-sea fishing, golf, mutual-fund investing, kite flying, fine wine, cooking, genealogy, the internet, magic, juggling, motivational speaking, playing the bagpipes, and coaching soccer for a team of six-year-olds. It's a system that builds confidence a step at a time, letting you progress rapidly from gathering information to hands-on experi-mentation. It breaks down like this:

Reading is the layman's doorway to the history, principles, and language of any given subject of inquiry. It's a way to find out what has worked before and what hasn't. By exposing yourself to different opinions and a wide range of views, you can triangulate from one to another and begin to develop your own perspective. You can build a pile of pros and cons to sort through. Remember that there are absolutes—such as, murder is wrong. But in many instances, "truth" is a relative concept. "Truth" often depends on how well you can argue your case.

Talking refines a sense of context for your subject. It's a way to develop a gut feeling for the relative value of the principles you've read about. Talking provides an immediate back-and-forth forum for gauging the relevance of the information you've gleaned in your reading. Talking gives you direct answers to your direct questions. Like a newspaper reporter, ask every question that occurs to you. Gather every tiny scrap of information, no matter how minor it may seem.

Note: If you've absorbed what you've read, you'll be better equipped to ask actionable questions and understand the answers.

Trying is how you gain experience. This is where it all comes together. Don't underestimate the power of experimentation. It adds to your knowledge in a way no amount of reading and talking can do. But to get the most from your experimenting, you need to build a context for it. You need the grounding that reading and talking provide.

Here's how you might apply *Reading, Talking, and Trying* to your life. Let's say you're half of a working couple with one spouse who wants to write a letter of resignation and return to school.

Draw three vertical columns on a sheet of paper. Label the first *Reading*, the next *Talking*, and the last *Trying*. Let's look at identifying ways to resolve the unknowns you face.

Under *Reading*, list all available sources of written information—from government documents to the Internet to the local public library. You or your spouse want to go back to school, but you're not sure you have the money. So you might read a few books about budgeting your limited resources. You might send away for information about student loans and scholarships.

Under *Talking*, list anyone you know or could get to know who might help you refine your perspective. You might talk to people who've done what you're thinking of doing. You might talk to the personnel director where you work to find out about opportunities for part-time jobs or tuition reimbursement programs.

Under *Trying*, list the kinds of tests you might try on a small scale that address elements of the unknown. You could try living on one income for a few months to see if what works out on paper will be acceptable to you in reality.

Read about it, talk about it, then give it a try—one toe at a time, if you feel more comfortable that way. Once you realize you've taken concrete steps to deflate some of the mystery from the unknown, your fear of the unknown will begin to wither away to nothingness.

Once You See It,
You Can Be It

*Courage is a willingness for adventure; a
willingness to go where life takes you; a
willingness to enjoy life even when times
are tough.*

ELLEN GUIDERA, AGE 38

When you're getting ready to take that first step into the
unknown, visualizing yourself succeeding helps in building your momentum. Imagine the ball falling through
the hoop; feel yourself getting a good start off the block; picture
your boss agreeing that, yes, you *do* deserve a raise.

As your thoughts go, so goes your body. If you can visualize victory in your mind, you can achieve it. When you visualize and
think positively, you fuse your conscious and unconscious energies into a singular mission. If you can't see yourself succeeding,
it's far more likely you'll fail.

Visualized courage has an emotional quality. Like the wind,
you can't touch it. You can only feel it. It feels like a surge of energy coursing through your body. It makes you want to get out of
bed in the morning. It fills you with an eager sense of anticipation
for the day.

Like fear, negative visualization has an impact that's more than
just mental. When you're gripped in negative visualization, your

mouth is dry and your hands tremble. If you laugh, it's a nervous laugh. And continued exposure to negative visualization, like fear, can result in serious medical conditions.

My good friend, Joel Miller, inspired the following three-step visualization process:

1. *Imagine experiencing the trappings of success.* Imagine the smiles, the thanks, the congratulations, the applause, and all the feelings of having succeeded. Picture yourself standing in the winner's circle, and hold tightly to the feeling of having arrived at success.

2. *Mind walk backward one step at a time.* Rewind your mental tape from victory to your current position. What was required at each step? Build in your mind a wave of success that smooths out the fear bumps from your position to ultimate success.

3. *Take the crucial initial step forward.* With the feeling of success providing your motivational fire, move ahead to victory. The key to your journey is feeling in your heart that you've already arrived before you've started.

Negative visualization isn't always instantaneous. It often simmers quietly over time. Sometimes, negative images take months, years, and entire lifetimes to develop and grow.

When you aren't countering a negative fear, you're nurturing it. The time you postpone dealing with your thoughts is time you're allowing them to sink roots in your mind. In time, even a tiny, totally irrational fear can grow into a raging fear dragon that can cripple you as effectively and completely as a set of steel manacles. Years of feeling that you're stupid, ugly, or inept can stifle your ability to live life to its fullest.

Be alert to your negative images. Keep a close inventory of them. When you feel a new unfounded negative stereotype come into being in the back of your mind, go after it. Expose it, dissect it, familiarize yourself with it, and find out what gave rise to it in the first place.

My livelihood depends on my ability to inspire creative thoughts. I've worked hard to train my mind to make new associations and develop new ideas quickly and efficiently. This ability can create wonderful inspirations. It can also turn against me, resulting in potentially crippling negative images. The dark side of creativity is the propensity for fears to grow into paroxysms of self-doubt and second-guessing. For me, the best way to prevent a fear from multiplying is to throttle it in the cradle. When you're confronted with a sudden negative thought, your instinctive response is of critical importance. In my case, a half dozen deep breaths have a way of bringing me to a point of calm and stability. When a negative thought appears, I've learned to let it roll off me, like water rolling off a rock in a stream.

A life journey is like a stream. We can't control much of what happens around us, but we can control how we react to it. We can waste energy trying to break through the rocks that crop up in the flow, or we can roll off them and move on down the stream.

Visualization works, but it works better when your mind is calm. An anxious, discontented disposition is no match for fear. Sometimes, you have to will yourself to relax. Sometimes, you have to retreat to a place in your mind where you can find peace. It's a matter of programming your thoughts. You can program yourself to be brave and confident. Or you can predispose yourself to despair. Try this:

Program yourself for fear. Drum up some negative thoughts. Say "incompetent," "scared to death," "I'll never make it," "it's hopeless." A good friend, Chic Thompson, has compiled an exhaustive list of negative thoughts in his book, *"Yes, But . . .": The Top 40 Killer Phrases and How You Can Fight Them*. Here are a few: "The competition will eat you alive," "It's against company policy," "You'll offend too many people," "We've always done it this way," "It'll never work," "You're over the hill," and "You're too young." You get the idea. As you repeat your mantras of negativity, clench your fists, your toes, your jaw, your body. Focus on failure. Draw a picture in your mind of disaster.

Stop. That's enough. How do you feel? Lousy, right? You've just consciously dabbled in what millions of people do every day without thinking about it when they condition their bodies and minds for failure. Dr. Peale suggests you can take a similar approach to get the opposite effect. Try repeating words like "tranquillity" and "serenity." Picture a serene scene—a placid body of water, a purple mountain vista, a glorious sunset. Think of a place you've been—a place where you have golden memories. It might be a tropical island, the subway ride to Brooklyn, or the attic of your childhood home. My grandmother focuses on the heavens—deep blue from horizon to horizon during the day and filled with vivid constellations at night.

I hone in on one of two places—the far end of the lake at Boy Scout Camp Carpenter in Londonderry, New Hampshire, where I used to go on overnight canoe trips, or the top of a certain cliff above New London Bay on Prince Edward Island in Canada, where I vacation with my family. The thought of either locale calms me and restores a sense of well-being. I can almost smell the air, feel the sun and lose myself in the natural beauty. From this calm comes renewed equilibrium that leads to quiet sort of confidence that makes the impossible suddenly seem possible.

Long-term visualization is a vital function of long-term

health. But I've also applied the power of visualization to solving short-term, high-intensity challenges. Each week, I'm faced with the task of coming up with ideas for a wildly diverse range of client corporations, all under harsh time constraints. Sometimes, for whatever reason, I have difficulty coming up with just the right ideas. In such situations, with my back against the wall, I visualize myself coming up with all kinds of ideas. I call it focused daydreaming. Instead of thinking about deadlines and letting my head fill with fear-induced thoughts—such as, "The client's going to hate this" or "Is that the sound of my brain shutting down?"—I close my eyes and focus my thoughts on the concept of The Ultimate Idea. It's as if I go into a trance. I make my mind as quiet as possible, removing all conscious distractions, all thoughts of anything external. Then I tune down a few frequencies to my subconscious mind, where I can't hear, smell, or feel anything around me. I'm aware only of my goal and the fact that it's out there, shimmering just beyond the horizon. I just haven't spotted it yet. I climb up inside the problem and feel around in the dark. I imagine it in 3-D.

Almost every time, a solution reveals itself. My subconscious mind unveils a piece of an answer. I tug at the piece and, pretty soon, I'm riding along on an avalanche of momentum. With a clear vision of the beginning—of nothingness, really—the blockage is dissolved. And the problem is solved.

Humor is also a wondrous way to do battle with negative thinking. By their nature, negative images and thoughts tend to be overly serious and self-important. If you can exaggerate, satirize or otherwise make fun of negativity, it usually shrivels into the background. Phil Gates is a case in point of someone who used humor to defeat negative thinking.

Phil was at a point in his life where he was learning there were definite disadvantages to being blind. For one thing, you have to deal with the awkward fears and feelings people sometimes have when they're around someone who is blind. But Phil discovered he could help people feel more comfortable with his blindness if he could make them laugh.

"It puts people at ease if I joke about it," he said. "Like if someone says, 'You look good, Phil.' I'll say, 'Yeah? So do you. Did you get a haircut or something?'"

One day when Phil was thirty-two years old, the blood vessels inside his eyes ruptured. He could still see, but his vision was clouded with squiggly black lines. A few months later, he was blind.

"I remember thinking 'I can't live this way,'" he said. "I hated depending on other people. All of a sudden, I couldn't do much of anything for myself. I needed help to go anywhere. As a result, my friends started treating me more like a baby, less like a friend. And I was thinking it was going to be like this the rest of my life."

Many of his friends began thinking the same thoughts about him. Their negative feelings fed on his. It worked the other way around, too—until his life became one dark feeding frenzy of negativity. It would have stayed that way, probably, had Phil not taken a hard look at himself and come to the realization that he was such a pathetic sad sack, it was almost funny. Indeed, he would later say, it *was* funny. He held on to that. He used it. And in humor, he found a new resiliency—and a way to rebuild his life. He struck up new friendships, found new ways to approach life, made bold plans.

It was a challenge getting people to accept him on his own terms. But once he began taking steps, he found himself propelled forward by his own momentum and his natural sense of humor. He was planning to go back to school, maybe pursue a career in computers. It was a scary thought, he said—the idea of being totally blind, navigating a big campus. "My biggest fear was of failing," he said.

"But I had two choices. I could do nothing and not fail. Or I could take the risk and do something. And they say you learn from your failures."

The other point Phil considered was that, on a big college campus, he'd probably run into a lot of women. He might not see them, but he'd know they were there. And he was going to make sure they knew he was there. "I was always willing to go out on a blind date," he said.

Take a moment to reflect on the person you were before you picked up this book. On which side of the continental divide between a positive outlook and sheer negativity did your thoughts fall? Did you approach your life journey with positive thoughts that generate confidence, hope and courage? Or did you see only the dark side and, for the sake of avoiding disappointment, expect only the worst?

Think about the components of your life. Do you approach some with positive thoughts and others with negative images? What common threads run through your thoughts? Where do you find hope? What makes you feel negative?

What feeds your personality? Do you dwell on insecurities, stereotypes, prejudices, and the negative experiences of the past?

Or are the thoughts that define you aimed at doing, challenging, risking, and achieving?

Fear Is Relative,
So Use Relativity to Defeat It

*No matter how badly I feel or how bad my problems
are, when I get a phone call and someone says "How
are you doing?" I tell them how busy I am and how
well off I am to be in my own home, at 88. Then they
go on to tell me their troubles, and I feel small thinking about my problems.*

HAZEL HALL, AGE 88

The room is hushed. Everyone's face is pointed sharply at you, like an audience of hatchets. You're at the podium, ready to speak. Sweat flows in hot rivulets through your hair, behind your ears, down your collar. You feel like there's a tennis ball in your throat. You wish you could transfer the moisture in your palms to your parched lips.

You're a little nervous. That's a good sign. Being nervous means you're pushing back your fear frontiers. Having the jitters keeps you alert, awake, and generally heightens perception. Just don't let it go too far.

As you stand at the podium, focus on the relativity of your fear. Remember how easy it was when you were presenting your speech to your bathroom mirror or in your car on the way to work. You knew what you were doing. You've practiced. It's the same speech. All that's changed is your environment. Your fears are relative to the environment—they really have nothing at all to do with what you're about to say. You know what to say. So say it!

Okay, okay. I understand the environmental difference between addressing a conference room full of hatchet heads and watching your lips move in the reflected image of a foggy bathroom mirror. Relative environment dramatically colors the way we react in relative situations. A shift in frame of reference automatically changes our point of view. Hitting fungoes in batting practice and hitting hardballs in the bottom of the ninth with the score tied feel like two extremely different experiences.

When the environment has the potential to distract you from your task, go back to the basics. Fill your mind with fundamentals and push your fear of the setting out of your mind. Turn to your roots for perspective.

Before speaking to an audience, I take off my shoes. It's a practice that dates back to when I performed in magic and juggling shows throughout New England. I'd move around quite a bit. In bare feet, I was able to find the edge of the stage, the flatbed or the bandstand.

Being barefoot is my way of turning to my roots. The more I can be who I really am, the more likely I am to deliver a message aligned with my values and style. What started out as a way to keep my bearings has become a trademark. From the *Washington Post* to NBC News to CNN, the media have turned my barefoot approach to public speaking into a symbol of my countercorporate style.

To whatever extent possible, control the time, place, and environment in situations where you're likely to feel fear. For example, say, when you're proposing marriage. I've proposed only once. At the time, I was a little nervous. So I choreographed the whole thing ahead of time. I proposed to my wife at Greely Park in Nashua, New Hampshire. We were sitting on a blanket under a large willow tree. I poured champagne into a Waterford crystal glass. When she wasn't looking, I dropped the engagement ring into the glass. Then I handed her the glass and made my pitch. As it turned out, I didn't need the champagne or the Waterford. But why take chances? Besides, it helped me get the momentum rolling.

Think about it:

- What are the trademarks of your life, the small things you do that exemplify who you are?
- How can you use your personal trademarks to remain natural, real, and relaxed under pressure?
- How can you subtract the stress from stressful environments so you can perform to your potential?

I was reminded of the impact environment can have on one's outlook one summer when I traveled with friends to a lake in Indiana to fulfill my "open water" dive requirement to become certified as a scuba diver. You know how sometimes you get a wild, irresistible impulse? That's what scuba diving was for me.

Over each of the previous five weeks, I'd taken two hours of classroom scuba instruction, followed by two tightly supervised hours of diving class in a pool. The instructor, Curt Hashman, drilled us repeatedly on the minute details of the science of scuba diving, testing our knowledge on paper in the class and again in the cozy confines of a heated pool which, at its deepest, was only eight feet. By the time the last class arrived, all of us in the class— including Sandie Glass, her husband, Brad, and David Wecker— had gotten to the point where we treated our instructor with a touch of irreverence, so confident were we in our scuba skills. "Yes, Mr. Hashman—right away, Mr. Hashman," we would say in our patronizing way.

Then we hit the lake. It wasn't so big as lakes go—basically circular and 150 yards wide. A long time ago, it was a limestone quarry, abandoned when the quarriers reached the aquifer and the hole they'd mined began filling with water. Because of its steep limestone walls and limestone bed, the visibility was remarkably clear for fresh water, which made it ideal for diving. The lake's owners have turned it into a sort of underwater amusement park, sinking a variety of attractions under its glassy surface for fledgling scuba divers to explore—among them, an old school bus, an ancient panel truck, a skiboat, and a motorcycle.

We stood at the edge of this body of water in our frogman gear one sunny morning in June. Curt adjusted our weights until we achieved neutral buoyancy, then ordered us to swim to a buoy that marked a steel platform twenty-five feet beneath the surface, where we were to perform the tasks required for us to receive certification. He reminded us a half dozen times that, come what may, we were to remain relaxed and breathe normally. "Blah, blah, blah," we thought to ourselves. We'd heard it all before. Did Curt Hashman take us for idiots?

In pairs, we were given the signal to release the air in our inflatable diving vests and descend to the steel platform. Suddenly, in these new surroundings, every bit of information I thought I knew about scuba diving emptied itself from my head. Instead of the cool blue walls of a pool, I was looking into pale green water that seemed to stretch on forever in every direction. And I was looking at fish. There were no sharks, of course—mostly bluegills and a few largemouth bass. But they seemed like wild animals to me, capable of inflicting who knew what sort of damage. They were brazen, too, swimming right up to my mask. I was in their element, not mine.

I tugged at the gizmo that released the air in my vest. To my surprise, I remained submerged only about a foot beneath the surface. I was supposed to sink. So I reached for the rope that connected the buoy to the steel platform beneath me and tried as best I could to haul myself downward.

All four of us were having trouble descending. Sandie was so buoyant in her neoprene wetsuit that she reminded the rest of us of one of those huge, helium-filled cartoon balloons in the Macy's Thanksgiving Day Parade, the kind that have to be held down by sturdy men at the ends of long ropes to keep from drifting away.

We turned to our instructor with renewed respect. He explained that the environment of the lake had made us nervous and that, as a result, we were breathing in short, fast spurts. We weren't giving our lungs a chance to empty. Without exhaling all the way before taking in the next breath, our lungs were behaving like buoys. We needed to slow down, take a deep breath, let it out all the way—and relax. It required a conscious effort, but after a few minutes, we settled down to the point where we could descend to the steel platform.

The first test was to remove our masks underwater, let them flood with water, put them back on and, exhaling through our noses, blow out the water so that, once again, we could see clearly. When it was my turn, my pulse was pounding like a jackhammer. I felt myself starting to float toward the surface. I completed the test in a panic. Then I flippered backwards as best I could, hovered a foot over the platform and watched my classmates. They, too, were consumed with underwater angst. It didn't make sense. We'd all performed the exercise dozens of times in the pool. The only difference was that there were fish in the old limestone quarry. And a lot more water.

It took three more dives for us to earn certification. Each time, as we became more familiar with the environment, we removed a pound or two from our weight belts. All because we relaxed and slowed our breathing to a more normal pace.

Strap on your tank and think about it:

- Which environments are most comfortable for you?
- In what kinds of environments do you feel like a fish out of water?
- Does it make sense for you to feel this way?
- What can you do to isolate your task from your immediate surroundings?
- When you're in a setting that fills you with fear, what can you do to put yourself in a place that rekindles your confidence?
- What can you do to restore your sense of who you really are and what you really know is true?

Examine the challenges your environment presents. Divide them into their components. Remember that environmental fears are all relative. The first time you try something new in a new setting, it will probably be a scary experience. But with each new attempt, the environment will seem to become increasingly tame—even though the environment itself won't have changed at all.

Think back. What once frightened you that, today, presents no challenge whatsoever?

Remember, too, that everyone's reaction to fear and environment also is relative. What is frightening to one person may be run of the mill to the next. Tom Fox is a case in point.

Tom was seventeen years old before he embarked into the real world on his own. On the morning he was to fly solo for the first time, this is what he was told he'd have to do: He would have to walk by himself to the bus stop at Madison Road and Eastwood Drive in Cincinnati, where he would have to catch the Queen City Metro No. 554 and ride it for two miles, until it arrived at the IGA supermarket in suburban Oakley. At that point, he would have to remember to get off the bus. Then he'd have to find a phone and call the number to Bobbie Fairfax School, one of three schools operated by the Hamilton County Board of Mental Retardation and Developmental Disability, where Tom was a senior-level student. Once he'd checked in with his teacher, he was to continue on into the store. In the pocket of his green Charlotte Hornets Starter jacket were photographs of two products—Sun Light dish detergent and Cut-Rite wax paper. He would have to use the photos to locate the items on the shelves. Then he would have to take them to a checkout line, purchase them and count his change. Finally, he was supposed to carry his purchases out of the store. He would have to look both ways before crossing Madison Road on the WALK light. There, he would have to catch the bus that took him, the dish detergent, and the wax paper back to Bobbie Fairfax.

One of Tom's teachers was Dave Kempton. Dave had been working with Tom for two years to get him ready for his first solo flight in a real world environment. In the early stages of environmental training, a small group of students and a staff member would take short trips on the bus. Maybe they'd go downtown or to the Oakley branch library or to the IGA to pick up stuff for the home-living teacher to use to make cookies. Each trip was aimed at warming the students up to the idea of going somewhere and doing something on their own. Once the students had a feel for being out and about, their small group would be dispatched on missions of its own, with the staffer following at a respectable distance in a car. After that, the students who took to it would be allowed to go on their first solo flights—again, with Dave or another staffer trailing behind, at least initially.

Environmental training isn't for everyone. A student has to know how to use a pay phone and have arrived at the senior level, which means he or she is ready to go find a job, either at one of the board's five adult workshops or out in the world at large. But Tom was ready. He hoofed it the half mile from the school to the bus stop. When he stepped off the bus at the Oakley IGA, he stood on the sidewalk for a moment, rubbing his chin thoughtfully, never noticing Dave waiting in his car in the parking lot.

Tom needed a little help calling the school. But that wasn't his fault, seeing as how the plastic card with the school's number was prefixed with the area code. That confused him for a moment. But he found the detergent and the wax paper. He handed the clerk $3 and accepted six cents in change.

"Bye," he told the clerk. "Good-bye," the clerk told him. And as he stepped out of the Oakley IGA into the bright light of a spring day, his grocery sack under his arm, it dawned on him that, hey, he'd done something here. Something that would affect the rest of his life.

For Tom, the simple act of navigating in the world for the first time—taking the bus, crossing the street, making a phone call, and picking up a few items at the grocery store—was a stunning personal triumph. Imagine how intimidating that first time was for Tom. Consider how his first solo flight was broken down into individual steps, one at a time. Think about the victories you could achieve if you took that same approach.

High anxiety happens. It's altogether reasonable in certain surroundings to have a stomach full of butterflies. What matters is how you deal with your fear in hostile environments. It's your choice. You can let your surroundings be dead ends, or you can re-duce them to minor obstacles that have to be swept away so you can resume your journey.

Your fears may never leave you, no matter how frequently you face them. What will change is your ability to synthesize them, manage them, put them into perspective, and transform them from liabilities into assets. When you can turn a fear into an as-set, you'll nudge the boundaries of your fear frontier outward. You'll find yourself seeking greater and greater challenges. And you'll grow.

Sometimes, you'll succeed. Sometimes, you won't. The fact is, the only way to discover what's beyond the edge of the cliff is to step over it from time to time. Most people, because of their all-encompassing fear, never find out what's beyond the edge. Most people are edge avoiders who play not to lose, instead of playing to win.

When you learn to juggle, the concept of "the edge" is always on your mind. No matter how much you practice, there's always another trick out there that's just beyond your grasp—a trick that, whenever you attempt it, leaves you scrambling to pick up your pins, bowling balls, or flaming torches. That's okay. That's life. Live it. Don't be afraid to look over the edge. Because each time you do, your courage will grow.

Think about it.

How often do you put yourself at the edge? Can you imagine using the exhilaration you feel when you're standing at the edge to generate courage? In what legs of your life journey do you play not to lose when you should be playing to win?

If you were to step over the edge, what's the worst that could happen? Is it really worth worrying about?

Facing Your Fear Dragons

*Courage is simply a matter of when your body
says "I can't," your heart and mind take over
and say "you will."*

JOE DREITLER, AGE 45

Even small fears can become nasty fire-breathing fear dragons that can fill your head, incinerate your confidence and
seize control of your thoughts. But by no means are they invincible. Like all dragons, they exist only in your imagination. You
have the power to make them grow or shrink. You create your own
fear dragons. You can claim dominion over them, too. But you
have to keep at it, because it's a continuing process.

The first step in dealing with fear dragons is to identify them.
Give them names, study their habits, get to know their character-
istics. For all their power, fear dragons are shy creatures. Many disappear when you drag them into the light of day. Others vanish
when they hear you talking openly about them with others. But
sometimes, it's difficult to track the dragon to its source. That's
because our own shadows wrap us in darkness.

A quick, easy way to pinpoint the origin of a fear dragon is to
talk about it with someone you trust—someone with an independent perspective. When I feel a fear dragon growing in the back of

my mind, I'll seek my wife's guidance. Amazingly, Deb usually slays my dragons with a few well-placed words. She'll make some simple, commonsensical observation that hasn't occurred to me. Or she'll explain why my thinking is faulty or my worrying unfounded. Or she'll show me why my dragon is often nothing more than a puff of smoke.

If, after consulting with others, you come to the conclusion that your dragon has a valid reason for being, the best way to fight it is to confront it directly. Look it straight in the eye and, more often than not, you'll send it running for cover. But beware—fear dragons have great patience. If you let them be, they'll wait you out every time. Simply trying to put them out of your mind seldom makes them disappear.

One of my daughters confronted a fear dragon head-on when she was in kindergarten. A boy her age teased her all the time. Whatever she did, whatever she said, whatever she wore, he teased her about it. He traveled in a pack, like boys do, so she felt bullied. She became afraid of him. Sooner or later, she knew she'd have to face him. But how?

One afternoon, she and I were discussing her dilemma at my office. Miki Reilly, who worked with me at the time, offered a plan. The next morning, when the boy began his daily litany, my daughter walked up to him and, in a voice loud enough for all to hear, said, "The reason you tease me is because, really, you like me." Yikes! In an instant, the monster turned into a mouse. His pack of friends turned on him. The teaser became the teasee. And that was the end of my daughter's problem.

Fear dragons can flourish in a vast range of territories. There's the fear of aging, rejection, making decisions, being laughed at, death, your children leaving home, striking up a conversation with someone you find yourself attracted to, ending a relationship, embarrassment. Fears tend to travel in packs, too—most of us are dealing with more than one fear at any given time. Add them all together, and it's no wonder some people end up feeding and nurturing an entire den of dragons.

A particularly paralyzing example is the fear of what others think of you. The irony is that, usually, the same people are just as concerned about what you think of them. It strikes me as odd that all that bipolar worrying doesn't cancel itself out. But it doesn't. So we live our lives through the expectations of someone else—be it a parent, a boss, an accountant, or a lawyer, all probably well-intentioned people with what they believe to be our best interests at heart—but people whose beliefs and frames of reference are nonetheless wildly out of sync with who we really are. Too often, out of a misguided sense of obligation or responsibility or fear or disillusionment or discouragement, we do what they say.

If that's what you're doing, stop it. Right now. Even if you don't have a viable alternative at the moment. Because you'll find one soon enough. And because no one has the right to be your master. That's *your* job.

My grandfather once told me about Rob Booth of South Livermore, Maine. Someone asked Rob one year how he was able to continue farming, considering there'd been so much rain in the spring, followed by so little rain in the summer that his crops had practically turned to dust.

"We make do," Rob replied. "When I go to bed so discouraged, fearful for our farm's survival, I dwell on what we can do and what we can't do. Then I realize I can't solve anything tonight. So I close my eyes, and I go to sleep."

Rob knew how to tame his dragons—just as you can control how you react to what's going on in your mind. Because the only way a fear dragon can grow is if you allow it to grow.

*   *   *

Here's a story about someone who wiped out an entire herd of fear dragons practically overnight when she stopped worrying about what other people thought about her. And once she stopped worrying, she began to blaze some serious trails.

Betsey Freiburger is thirty years old, five-foot-ten and is what they call in department-store parlance "full-figured," "big-boned," "a plus size." After dozens of attempts at dieting with varying levels of success, Betsey came to a point in her life where she decided she wasn't a size 6 screaming to get out of a size-whatever body. She decided she was all right the size she was.

If there was a turning point, that was it. It took courage for Betsey to arrive at that decision. It meant no longer being afraid of being snickered at for who she was. Her next move was a clear statement that she was no longer afraid of what people might think of her.

She entered a contest sponsored by *BBW*—short for *Big Beautiful Woman*—magazine. Something like 30,000 women entered, and Betsey won. She did her best Kim Basinger for *BBW*'s June '93 cover. These days, Betsey makes a living modeling clothing for women who have only recently been getting attention from the fashion industry; women for whom designers have finally looked beyond the milieu of muu-muu'd matrons into the zone of duds that have—dare I say it?—sex appeal. It's a good living, too. Betsey and her full figure draw up to $1,250 a day.

Nowadays, Betsey is aiming for a cover on one of the mainstream fashion magazines—perhaps draped in a flamboyant Christian LaCroix original, maybe showing a little too much cleavage from the cover of *Vogue* or *Elle*.

Think about it. When your friends and family are filing past your casket at the funeral home, how do you want to be remem-

bered? Do you want to be remembered as someone who flour-
ished despite the rocks, hurdles, and hardships life threw at you?
Or do you want to be remembered as someone who never made
much of an impression on anybody; that is, do you want to be remembered at all?

Consider the content of your life and how you approach living.
You can't always control your circumstances, but you can control
how you react to them. You can't change where you came from,
but you can change where you are now. And you can set a course
for where you go from here.

Send Your
Fear Dragons Running

Courage is standing behind your guns. Especially when they're not really loaded.

MATT NEREN, AGE 22

Pruning dead branches helps a tree grow. We have branches, too, that require pruning from time to time. They're the deep-seated prejudices we impose on ourselves and accept from others about exactly what we can and cannot do.

Perhaps you need to do some pruning. What preconceptions do you have about your abilities? When you were in school, did you get a few bad grades in a certain subject and immediately assume you had no talent in that area? Did one inept teacher or one bad experience create in you a personal prejudice that you weren't good at math, couldn't write a complete sentence, or would never excel in science?

Early on, I developed two particularly tenacious fear dragons that controlled me in dramatic ways. Over time, I came to accept as absolute truths the premises that (a) I couldn't write and (b) I had a genetic defect that made it impossible for me to learn other languages. It was clear to me I just wasn't a verbal person—not on paper, at least.

Based on standard grading systems, I was good at math and science, but I would never be a writer. Writing petrified me. Whenever I had a writing assignment in school, I anticipated and received negative feedback. I worked diligently at avoiding formal writing in any form.

I was so intimidated by this particular fear dragon that, when it came time to declare a major at the University of Maine, I settled on chemical engineering, in part because Chem E majors were required to have the least number of English and writing credits. I knew this because I'd gone through the college syllabus and counted the number of English classes required for the various majors that interested me.

When a self-imposed prejudice sinks roots in your mind, it's quite painful. Like an alcoholic, you go to extremes to avoid being exposed. You're terrified people will find out how ignorant you think you are—and that they'll agree. You may even elicit support from others to enable your phobia. When group projects would be assigned in school, I'd offer to handle the oral presentation as long as my teammates did the writing. In retrospect, I know now that my teammates were as frightened at the prospect of speaking in public as I was of writing. Public speaking, I could do. So I focused on that. It wasn't rational. Deep-seated fear dragons never are. The words would come to me when I was standing in front of an audience, but never when I was staring at a blank sheet of paper.

As the years passed, I confirmed and reconfirmed my lack of writing ability. The fear dragon had taken over completely, to the point that I looked for reasons to justify my fears. Teachers would write constructive comments on essays and term papers, and I would react defensively. Instead of looking at their comments as opportunities to learn and grow, I used them to validate my prejudice.

I let the dragon grow for more than fourteen years, from the second grade until college graduation. It took at least that long to slay it.

My first boss at Procter & Gamble helped me see things differently. She pointed out that, while it was true I didn't have much grasp of the mechanics of spelling, punctuation, and syntax, I was able to develop a persuasive, cogent argument. For the first time, I saw a glimmer of a vision as to how I might be a writer after all.

Today, I feel fairly well freed from that particular fear dragon. It's what I do for a living. The process wasn't easy, but it was worth the effort. One of these days, I'll deal with that "genetic" defect that makes it impossible for me to learn other languages. Like, say, French. Now that I'm of legal drinking age, I've developed a taste for French wines. Knowing the language will come in handy when I fulfill a dream and visit the vineyards of Bordeaux.

Stop a moment and think. What are your fear dragons? Over the years, what personal prejudices about yourself have you come to accept as true? What are you convinced is impossible for you to do? What's the source of this belief? What experiences brought you to this conclusion? What do you think you "know" about yourself that, in reality, you never can truly know?

How have you allowed this "knowledge" to hold you back on your life's journey?

It's always been acceptable, if not rational, to be afraid of anything new. In today's world, this is especially true of new technology. The prospect of having to face new technology is a classic fear dragon. Culturally, it has become socially acceptable to joke about our inability to program a VCR to record or boot a CD-ROM on a computer.

That's unwise. Today, it's grow or die. If you're not keeping pace with technology, you have no right to complain about your lack of progress, job satisfaction, or salary increases. Either learn about technology or go the way of the pterodactyl.

Technology is good. Technology means growth. But technology is about more than jobs—it's about making life more enjoyable. Most technologies empower the individual.

Most children have no fear of technology—unlike grownups, who often find it easier to say "I can't" than "I'll try." Children accept the fact that they'll fail, fail, and fail again before learning something new. As adults, we avoid the potential for failure. If we can't be assured of being 100 percent successful in the beginning, we'd just as soon not enter the starting gate.

Technofear is by no means exclusive to the Computer Age. Resistance to technology dates back to the time the first caveman tried to talk his contemporaries into cooking their kills instead of eating them raw.

My great-grandfather, William Holder, discovered as much more than 100 years ago. But he understood the importance of new technology and kept his courage. His father, George E. Holder, owned a sail-making shop in the New Brunswick harbor town of Saint John. His was one of dozens of shops that hand-crafted sails for the tall ships. The process was a long, arduous one—and my great-grandfather decided there had to be a better way to do it.

On a trip to New York City, he heard about a remarkable new machine that was especially designed for sewing sails. His father was against the idea. At that time in Canada, sail-making was considered a manly art. And sewing machines were for women.

Will didn't see it that way. Despite repeated objections, he talked his father into buying a couple of sewing machines as an experiment. It was the first time anyone had seen sewing machines in a Canadian sail loft, and the men who worked with Will didn't take kindly to them. The sailmakers' resistance ran so deep that Will agreed to pay them double to get them to learn to use the machines. He'd calculated that he'd get more than double their normal productivity once they became proficient on the machines.

At first, he was ridiculed around the Saint John waterfront. His competitors called him the "petticoat sailmaker." But while they were laughing at him, he was taking their business. He could produce a better, stronger sail with his sewing machines in a fraction of the time it took his rivals to hand-stitch their sails. And today, more than a century later, the George E. Holder & Son sign still hangs on Water Street in Saint John, the only one of the original sailmakers still in business.

The story of my great-grandfather is a treasured family legend. It inspired me early in my career at Procter & Gamble and gave me the courage to engage in one of my first corporate battles.

It was 1981. In my role as brand assistant in the marketing department, I was charged with compiling and assembling a massive collection of budget charts. This process required me to make 2,673 alterations and updatings in six months, which in turn required multiple all-nighters. Aside from being unbearably tedious, that aspect of the job struck me as a waste of time.

Having taken a number of computer courses as a chemical-engineering major in college, I'd come to believe that the computer's most basic application was to eliminate the need for people to perform tedious, repetitive tasks. The computer had the potential of doing for white-collar workers what the power saw and the belt sander had done for the carpenter. Computers could be tools for freeing the individual from process drudgery to allow more time for thinking, inspiration, and craftsmanship.

At school, I'd used a mainframe computer. But I'd heard about a company called Apple that had a computer that could run a program called VisiCalc, the first electronic spreadsheet to perform calculations and recalculations. As it happened, P&G's management-systems division had an Apple II computer. Working nights and weekends, I built a VisiCalc spreadsheet of the budget charts. Suddenly, what had been the most tedious part of my job was a simple matter of punching a few buttons when changes flowed down the management chain to me. It was fantastic. While my fellow brand assistants were grinding their fingers and their secretaries' fingers to nubs on manual calculators, I simply typed a few numbers into the Apple II and the job was done.

My only problem was that, for the most part, my access to the Apple II was limited to nights and weekends. I decided to see if the company would purchase one for my desk. My request slammed into a brick wall. What I was proposing had never been done. My enthusiasm was flattened under the steamroller of more mature, more professional advisors who told me that brand people didn't work on computers. They told me computers were for geeks. In fact, some colleagues suggested that, if I weren't careful, senior management might get the idea that I didn't belong in advertising brand management and reassign me to management systems.

They didn't get it. So I put together another proposal, showing that an assortment of tasks that normally took 231 hours and 30 minutes to perform with the traditional hand calculator could be accomplished in 30 hours and 21 minutes on an Apple II. This calculation was based only on my time. Once the time it took secretaries to retype the reports was factored into the equation, the savings were immense. I wrapped up the proposal with the story of the Petticoat Sailmaker, drawing parallels between the technofear my great-grandfather had encountered with my own experience with the Apple II.

The proposal was passed up the corporate food chain to the company's most senior executive committee, where it was decided to assign a test computer to the Coast Soap brand group under my care.

I couldn't have asked for better results. The brand had faster, more accurate numbers than ever before. I remember the newly converted office manager patting me on the back and predicting that one day, Procter & Gamble might have an Apple II on every floor. I hazarded a guess that, gee, who knew? We might even see a time when a personal computer would be a fixture on every desk. The office manager pulled his arm from around my shoulder, rolled his eyes ever so slightly, and grinned at my youthful exuberance. He walked away shaking his head.

He has since stopped shaking his head. Today, the thought of doing business without personal computers is too ridiculous to contemplate.

From sewing machines to personal computers to whatever advances are waiting to be discovered in the future, our collective bias against new technology will never go away. Anything new will always be viewed through the narrow eyes of suspicion. Challenging the established ways of thinking will always require courage. Bold new thoughts, no matter how visionary, are rarely received with standing ovations. But without bold new thoughts, we'd still be squatting in our caves, rolling our eyes and shaking our heads at the shaggy man in the cave next door who insists on holding the meat from his kill over a fire. Call it fear of technology or fear of any sort of change—in either case, it's a threat to our ability to enjoy life's journey to the fullest.

Think about it. When have you passed up a chance to shake up the status quo? Why? Do you still think it was the right thing to do? In what ways are you using old-fashioned approaches to avoid risking failure with new techniques? How have you avoided change, even when change could provide a solution?

Good Luck Comes
to the Dedicated

I've realized that to bring real meaning into my life requires having the courage to let things happen, not to just make things happen. It's a faith that by moving through life more consciously and gently, while holding fast to my standards and beliefs, I will make a real difference in our world.

CARLTON BRUEN JR., AGE 42

You've dedicated yourself to your cause. You've done everything you could think of—all you can do now is let luck take its course. And the only way luck can be of any help at all to you is if you're in the arena, taking chances. Because if you're sitting on the sidelines watching, luck doesn't matter.

Good luck comes to those who are dedicated to their mission. Rare indeed is the highly successful person who won't admit to having had his or her share of breaks—the operative words being "their share." Successful people know luck doesn't just happen; it's an ancillary benefit of being actively dedicated to a mission.

For instance, what are the odds you'll get lucky and find the job of your dreams if you spend all your time on the couch watching Country Music Television? Extremely slim, right? On the other hand, what are the odds of getting lucky and finding a job if every day for three months you mail out a half dozen resumes, knock on doors, and network with people who work in the area of your interest? There's no way to say for sure, but you can count on them being better than slim.

People ask how to sell an idea that's been kicking around in their heads. My first question is, who have they approached? More often than not, they haven't actually presented their idea to anyone. They've thought a lot about it, but haven't really done anything worth mentioning.

Hello? It's a universal law of creativity physics: you can't sell an idea—in fact, you can't make anything happen—unless you take tangible action. It's not enough simply to have an idea—you have to show it off to make it real.

The "You Can't Unless . . ." rule applies across all types of frontiers. You can't find a new job unless you apply for one; you can't improve communications with your teenager unless you're in the same room; you can't lose weight and stay healthy unless you exercise on a regular basis and make serious cutbacks in your Twinkie intake.

Having good luck is not necessarily a matter of winning the lottery. Good luck is what happens to people who work hard and take bold chances. The amount of good luck you have coming to you is in direct proportion to the number of chances you take. In any situation, you have an element of pure random chance. Sometimes, because of the way luck shakes out for you, you score a long string of successes or failures. Preparation, heart, faith, and commitment can reduce the percentage of your fate that is determined by pure chance, but they can't eliminate it.

Likewise, you can't plan for luck. Luck usually comes as a bolt out of the blue. But you can be ready for it.

You also have to let it happen. To do that, you have to believe. It helps to have a childlike faith in your mission. For children, believing in wonders and miracles comes easily. As we grow up, we become skeptical, mature, and increasingly inclined to decide that such and such a thing could never come to pass.

My children have made it their job to remind me that miracles happen regularly. They tend to bring up the fact in my moments of deepest frustration. And they say so with such total faith that it makes me stop and realize, hey, wait a minute—they're right! Whatever name you want to use—luck, kismet, simple twists of fate, miracles—they happen with such frequency that I wonder why we think of them as rarities.

As children, we believe in miracles. As adults, we discount possibilities. We put more faith in the bad than the good because, that way, we're less likely to be disappointed. To protect our delicate egos, we focus on one or two minor points that could go awry instead of working hard to enhance the odds that the larger picture will come into focus.

Richard Steineman's story is a parable of precisely the sort of good fortune that can occur when one is totally dedicated to a cause. One December day, Richard and his partner, the Reverend Mark Schneider, closed a $15,000 deal on a century-old, three-story brick house in what was, at the time, the bleakest slum in Cincinnati. Richard's plan was to bring the brick house up to code and call the place St. Joseph's House of Hospitality. It was to be a shelter for the homeless. His start-up budget was zero.

But he put everything he had on the line—his time, his energy, and what little worldly wealth he had. In the process, he began experiencing what he called "ordinary, everyday miracles." After a while, he almost came to expect them.

At first, the entire house was heated with a single small space heater. Richard's first four guests were expecting to spend a chilly night together that first evening. Suddenly, a man knocked on the door with three kerosene space heaters. Just like that. Richard had never seen the guy before.

A few days later, Richard began planning Christmas dinner for his guests, who by that time numbered ten. The only problem was, he didn't have a stove. All he had was a kitchen table and three space heaters. But he kept planning his dinner, as if its eventual reality was a foregone conclusion. "And wouldn't you know it—at 2 P.M. on Christmas Eve, a fellow called to tell me he had a blank check for me," Richard said. "So I ran out and found a good used stove for $125. A Magic Chef."

Out of the blue. The following month, it occurred to Richard that the kerosene heaters posed a fire hazard. He thought it would be a good idea to buy a furnace. He had only $38 in the bank, but he ordered the furnace anyway. Once again, he said, his dedication and his faith in God resulted in another miracle: "When the payment came due, I had the money. I guess word got out about what I was trying to do. And people just gave."

All this time, Richard was amazed at how things worked out, at how an ordinary miracle would come along just when he needed one.

Richard's story is no less amazing than the luck that ordinary, everyday people—those who have a genuine commitment to a cause—experience every day. It's not hard to dedicate yourself when you've taken up a challenge and you've racked up an unbroken string of successes. You're finding plenty of positive reinforcement—naturally, you'll have the energy to persevere. Dedication comes easily when the sun is shining, the waves are lapping at the beach and nothing stands between you and your piña colada.

Unfortunately, life doesn't dish up many such scenarios. It's another thing altogether to carry on when the world seems to have turned against you. Bad news can wear us out. Like water dripping on a rock, hardship and suffering slowly grind us down.

We become skilled craftspeople in the art of negative thinking. We batten down hatches and shut ourselves off from anything that might cause us short-term pain or embarrassment. Perpetuating sameness in your life is one way to avoid making mistakes, but you pay a price. You sacrifice the chance to learn how life works.

I've got to hand it to Norman Vincent Peale. He hit on something big when he came up with his positive thinking manifesto. When you're thinking positively, the world crackles with possibilities. Probably the best part about thinking positively is that it kindles courage. Positive thinking can't help but put you in a courage mode—almost without your having to think about it.

That's because when you think positively, you believe in yourself. And you're a whole lot more likely to risk failure in order to achieve. You see all the way to the end of the tunnel. You believe things will work out. And when you believe that, you have the courage to dedicate yourself despite a run of bad luck. This is the essence of courage.

Ted Geisel—we know him better as Dr. Seuss—was rejected by twenty-seven publishing houses when he tried to sell his first children's book, *And to Think I Saw It on Mulberry Street*. The publishers he'd seen all told him his manuscript was too unlike other children's books. Geisel was on the verge of giving up when his luck took a turn.

One day on a street in New York City, he happened to bump into a guy he'd gone to Dartmouth College with. In the course of conversation, the guy happened to mention he'd just started a new publishing house. Shortly afterward, Dr. Seuss was introduced to the world. Thank goodness for Geisel's luck that day. If not for that chance meeting with his old college pal, if he'd happened to be walking down a different street, if his pal had been a few minutes late getting back to his office, we might never have learned about the Grinch, the Cat in the Hat, or green eggs and ham.

Look at it this way—bad luck isn't necessarily a bad thing. Not at all. Bad luck can be a stepping stone to good luck. It can help build your courage. Because every time you pick yourself up, dust yourself off and try again, your resistance to fear increases. Besides, the more bad luck you have, the greater the odds become that, on your next attempt, you'll score a direct hit on your target.

Whenever I see a reporter on the 11 o'clock news interview a firefighter who's just pulled a child from a burning building, I react in wonder and admiration. Where did he—or she—find the courage to walk into a three-alarm fire? And then to walk out again—was that person lucky or what? But, you never see the hero in such stories gloat. The response is almost always something along the lines of "I was only doing my job." Right. But what a job!

Such high-hazard jobs obviously require deep personal courage. But these occupations also have some of the most effective preparation programs in the world. People regularly called upon to perform under dangerous circumstances undergo rigorous training. They read, study, attend lectures, and take test after test. They spend weeks and months in physical drills reviewing techniques they'll need to remain effective and in one piece. They practice the same moves, reactions, and procedures over and over again, until their reactions in specific situations are automatic and instinctive. Even after qualifying for field duty, they continue to work with veterans who observe, counsel, and refine as the rookies prepare to face real life-and-death scenarios.

It's all calculated to turn ordinary people into professionals who react instantly and instinctively under intense pressure. It drums out fear while drumming in courage and a propensity for lucky breaks. Luck, when it happens, doesn't simply occur for people who've been trained to deal with specific sets of circumstances; they're trained to be ready when luck opens one of its windows of opportunity. Through experience and training, they develop inner gyroscopes that keep them balanced and give them a clear understanding of what to do and what not to do in times of emergency, all of which opens luck's window that much wider.

You can expect the worst—in which case, you'll never be disappointed. Or you can hope for the best. When you dwell on the negative, you experience failure, pain and defeat in your mind over and over again. When you dwell on the positive, you experience the feeling of failure only once—and then, only if it actually occurs. If you believe in yourself, good things have a way of happening. If you let them.

Good luck also has a better-than-average chance of happening for those grounded in a solid system of values. As an Eagle Scout and long-time supporter of the Boy Scouts of America, I take particular pride in the story of Bryan Clark, a Cincinnati scout who had the courage to take action when the need arose—and the luck to be in the right place at the right time to save a life.

Like almost every other hero you've ever heard of, Bryan didn't think of himself as a hero; he saw himself as a normal fifteen-year-old kid for whom the time and place were right. But it took courage to do what he did—courage that was, in a way, trained into him. Bryan, who lives in Cincinnati, received the Scouts Honor Medal for risking his own life to rescue thirty-five-year-old Suzanne Peters from drowning in an undertow outside Panama City, Florida.

Bryan explained, "Five of us were swimming, maybe fifty yards out, and we realized the current was pretty strong. A seventh-grade girl in our group was having a little trouble, so Suzanne went to help her. The younger girl started to make it okay, but then Suzanne started swallowing water as the waves went over her head. She was calling for help, and I could barely see her head above the water. She was having a hard time getting her breath, gasping and all. So I swam out and brought her back. I grabbed her with one arm and swam with the other."

Suzanne told Bryan she felt as though she was given a second chance in life.

"You don't want to let something like that go to your head," Bryan said. "I felt like I had a duty to do what I could."

Train yourself to encourage your courage, and you'll increase the chances of good luck happening to you. Enhance your instinctive skills by practicing and preparing yourself for change.

Think about yourself. Are you fully dedicated to your cause or causes? Or are you coasting along on the surface praying for a random act of luck? Are you waiting for luck to happen or are you working to find it?

Listen to Your Heart

*When something hits you in the innermost part of
your being as totally wrong and you express your dis-
may, feeling everything you've always been brought up
to believe has been pushed aside, then you live with
dissension and sometimes isolation. But if it's right,
time will prove it.*

HAZEL HALL, AGE 88

Changing the world—even your small corner of it—is hard
work. You have to be motivated to make a difference. And
you need courage—more courage, maybe, than you think
you have. Otherwise, the first of the hundreds of obstacles you
confront will drop you like a bag of ball-peen hammers. The kind
of courage I'm talking about comes from the conviction you're
doing the right thing; the certainty that what you're setting out to
do will make the world a better place.

The purity of your motivation is vital to your success. Many
top companies emphasize the importance of doing the "right
thing in the right way." That core principle is presented as standard operating procedure to new recruits. I believe it's a big reason these companies are as successful as they are.

To find courage internally, your mission has to have significance. When your mission is pure and right, you won't have to
concern yourself with respect and financial reward. They'll be the
natural consequences of carrying out your mission.

We all run into fearful situations that provoke instant reactions. When a fire breaks out, when you get a call from the police notifying you of an automobile accident, when you get any kind of bad news, you have an instinctive response. You don't have time to think rationally. You can't break your fear apart and chew on it one piece at a time. Your response in times of trial flows from your values. Your reactions are based on your belief of what separates right from wrong.

Values take shape at an early age. At first, we get them from our parents, watching them interact with the world and learning how they define right and wrong. But as children, we have a way of testing our parents' instinctive reactions. Once, when my daughter, Tori, was two years old, we stayed at a hotel with an indoor swimming pool and all went swimming. When it was time to leave, I lifted each of my three children from the water and left them standing there while I walked around to the other side of the pool to get our towels. Suddenly, I heard a splash and the screams of Tori's older sister, Kristyn. Turning around, I saw Tori struggling underwater.

Time stopped. My instincts took control. I leaped into the pool with four towels, my wallet, and my glasses. I pulled a shaken, frightened little girl from the pool and gave her a big hug. As we were sitting there at the pool's edge, her crying turned to laughter.

"What?" I asked. She pointed to four towels, my wallet, and my glasses at the bottom of the pool.

My love for my child drove my reaction. In life, many of the sharpest, most sudden fears that leave little room for anything other than instinctive reactions can be addressed through your basic instincts of right and wrong.

One of the richest sources of courage is the fundamental belief in the rightness of your cause. This is the sort of courage Rosa Parks displayed in Montgomery, Alabama, on December 1, 1955, when she made her historic stand for the cause of civil rights. Rosa was taking the bus that day, as she did every other day. A white bus driver wanted her to move to the back of the bus with the other black passengers to make room for a white passenger.

She refused. In that one simple act, she changed America for the better and forever. Her arrest spurred blacks in Montgomery to boycott the bus service for 381 days, resulting in a Supreme Court ruling that made bus segregation unconstitutional. "I felt the Lord would give me the strength to endure whatever I had to face," she wrote in one of her books, *Quiet Strength: The Faith, the Hope and the Heart of a Woman Who Changed a Nation*. "God did away with all my fear. It was time for someone to stand up—or, in my case, sit down."

As a motivator, rightness of cause transcends the basic freedoms guaranteed under the Constitution. It extends throughout all aspects of our lives. It's easier, for example, to pursue an unpopular point of view if you think it's the right thing to do. The reason it's easier is that you have the courage of your convictions.

Let's say you're a member of a certain civic organization. Most of the members are interested in undertaking a certain fundraising project. But you genuinely believe it's not a wise course of action, based on real facts and your own experience. You're more likely to have the courage to stand up and speak your piece because your opinion is grounded in reality, rather than feelings, hunches, and conjectures.

When you're involved in a fearful situation that offers a number of options, listen closely to your heart. More often than not, a small voice inside you will tell you what's the right thing to do, even if the right thing is unpopular.

Values provide a framework for living. They make it possible to weigh options and make decisions you won't regret. When you make choices that are aligned with your values, you build your character and sense of self-worth. When you compromise your values, you're living a lie. The stronger your values, the more stable and secure you'll be.

In business and in life, success is a matter of meeting the customer's needs. Once, back when I was wrestling with whether to remain wrapped in the corporate cocoon or spread my wings and launch Richard Saunders International, I was invited to dinner by the vice president of what at the time was one of America's top marketing consulting firms, a concern based in southern Connecticut.

Over a meal at a fancy French restaurant where, in my opinion, the food was overpriced and the portions unforgivably skimpy, he described to me some of the ideas his company had turned, shaped, and spun into major success stories. I weighed his accomplishments against mine and concluded in my youthful exuberance that, considering the three board games I'd licensed and my performance working for corporate America, he and I were about even. So I asked him, "Sir, why should I come to work for you? Why shouldn't I work for myself?"

Because I didn't have any gray hair, he said. In this business, you are who you know, he said—not what you can do. Your Rolodex is more important than results, he said.

It was a pivotal moment for me—one that would play a large role in the success of Richard Saunders International. His blatant disregard for doing the right thing—delivering genuine, tangible results to customers—was most dismaying. I took it as a personal challenge to design a company that could deliver a better product and better service, with better timing and better results. His comment ran through my mind as I worked in my basement in the early days of my company, competing with big-time consulting firms. With that one dinner, Connecticut Man had provided me with a mission to enter a highly competitive field, despite my lack of both gray hair and an impressive Rolodex. And with that mission, he gave me courage.

As a postscript, Connecticut Man went on to become president of his firm. For six more years, he and his company continued not to do the right thing. And at the end of that time, his company was forced to file for bankruptcy.

You're you. That is, you're the sum of your personality, your upbringing, everything that has ever happened to you, and the ways in which you've reacted. Sometimes, when we align ourselves with a collection of people, our individual values become blurred. At its worst, we get swept up in what historians and newscasters call "mob mentality." Not all mobs parade around in brown shirts or stage spontaneous lynchings. Mobs aren't always so sinister. A mob might be a group of friends or a project team in a corporate setting. But whatever form it takes, the mere act of being part of one can wear away your identity. Because the natural tendency is to blend in, to run with the pack.

Working with some of the world's most high profile companies, I've found each has a distinct corporate psychology. The more successful a company is, the more its employees take on the mindset and values of that company while forsaking their own. In the process, they can lose a sense of self-worth. As a result, when the inevitable waves of downsizing and reengineering occur and these people receive pink slips, they tend to fall deeper into depression, wrapping themselves more tightly in self-pity than those with values and identities apart from their careers.

Again, you're you. You're not defined by your associates or

where you work. Never forget it. It's because of what you've done or haven't done that you're who you are and where you are. Your mother gave birth to you. To the best of my knowledge, no child has ever been born a corporate middle manager.

My eldest child, Kristyn, took a class in karate when she was eight years old. She was the only girl in a class of nine kids. The forces pulling at her to define herself in her classmates' terms were strong.

She was subjected to a lot of teasing from her classmates—mostly along the lines that girls had no business taking karate because girls couldn't do karate. She admits today they bothered her, but they also made her angry. She never considered quitting, though, because she was of the opinion her classmates were wrong. She was also of the opinion girls can do anything boys can do. And she'd decided it was up to her to impress her male classmates with that point.

As the class progressed, Kristyn concentrated on the instructor. When the boys were goofing off, she was learning. Before long, because she was paying attention, she was able to execute the moves as well, if not better, than many of the boys. The teasing died down.

The final class was Parents Observation Day. Having an audience put the boys in a mood to show off. One way to do this was to pick on the one kid in the class who was different from the rest, that being the girl. The teasing started up again in a big way.

The grand finale was this: Each student was supposed to break a board with a standing kick. Kristyn was feeling the pressure, having been reminded by her classmates that, as a girl, she'd never be able to perform the stunt. What they'd failed to take into account was the fact that she was driven by her sense of rightness—and her total conviction that splintering a piece of wood with her foot was perfectly within the bounds of her ability. In breaking that board, she would prove once and for all that girls could do anything boys could do.

The first boy broke the board. Despite several tries, the second boy didn't. Neither did the third. It was Kristyn's turn.

She focused every bit of training, concentration, and energy she had on that board, then booted it with everything she had. One kick was enough.

The room went quiet. Kristyn's classmates were too embarrassed to look at her afterwards. She didn't make a big deal about it; there was no need to. She'd made her point.

It was one of those moments that makes being a father the most satisfying job in the world.

Focus, Focus, Focus

The times I've found courage is when I've closed my eyes and looked into my soul. It's good to remember to stop at the heart to say hello.

EVAN OBRENTZ, AGE 39

When you look a fear dragon square in the eye, far more often than not, it will blink. After all, its veins are flowing with fear. And once you've got a fear dragon blinking, you're on the way to declaring victory. But you have to screw up a whole lot of concentration to look a fear dragon in the eye in the first place. You have to focus, focus, and focus some more, until your glare burns with a laser's intensity.

One effective method for honing, buffing, and otherwise enhancing your power of concentration is through competition. It's a matter of zeroing in for a short time on a single subject or task and focusing all your energy and thoughts on it. It's a kind of gamesmanship—or gameswomanship—so much so that some might consider it a kind of mind game. So what? Fear plays mind games with you. There's nothing wrong with turning the dragon's flame back on itself.

The thing about competition is, it can turn fear into fuel. The mere act of racing against time and around obstacles causes some sort of mental gland to kick in that zaps you with energy, which in turn adds to your courage quotient. Of course, the distinction between fear and exhilaration can be a fine line. Riding a roller coaster is scary and exciting. If you can channel your fear with a sense of adventure or competition, it quickly becomes exciting.

My children take riding lessons in the summer. The instructors use competition as a way to push back their students' fears.

When you're small, a horse's back is a long way from the ground. When you and your saddle weigh sixty pounds, a 1,300-pound horse can be awfully intimidating. It's hard to climb into the saddle. It's harder still to believe you can get your huge steed to turn to the left or the right with a touch of the reins. And it's almost impossible to imagine kicking your heels hard enough to make that big, strong horse break into a trot.

My children's instructors have a simple solution for helping kids overcome these fears. They divide the class into two teams and have a relay race. A student mounts his or her respective team's horse and races hell-for-leather to a galvanized steel tub filled with water and apples. The student dismounts, bobs for an apple, scrambles back into the saddle again, and races back to the starting point, where the next kid is waiting to run the course. The point is, the students are a whole lot more confident when they're competing than when they're not. In the heat of the competitive moment, they don't have time to hesitate.

In the same way, you can draw gumption from competing, both in your personal and professional lives. If you're a smoker who'd like to quit, you can compete with yourself to reduce the number of cigarettes you smoke each day by one or two until you arrive at zero. No matter what you're trying to accomplish, you can lose yourself—along with your feelings of inadequacy and fear—in the spirit of competition.

Probably without meaning to, at least at first, John Lennon and Paul McCartney drew from the competition that grew between them to write some of the most memorable music ever recorded. After Lennon's death, McCartney referred in numerous interviews to the competitive friction that drove their songwriting. After McCartney wrote "Yesterday," Lennon was spurred to write "Nowhere Man," which in turn prodded McCartney to write "Eleanor Rigby." Each became caught up in topping the other—and the world reaped the benefits.

The point of using competition is to distract yourself from negative thoughts and focus on the task at hand. And it works largely because competition counters that part of human nature that insists on overthinking a task or a fear. Competition limits choice. Competition puts you in a mindset that says "I have to." Granted, freedom of choice is a marvelous thing. But we can bog down with choices. We can also choose to be lazy.

Given too many choices, we can become too smart for our own good. Instead of instinctively responding to challenges, we sift our experiences through such filters as "Is it professional?" or "What will the neighbors think?" or "Someone like me has no business trying something like that."

Whether you perceive a risk as an opportunity or a reason to curl up into a ball of hopeless paralysis depends largely on your state of mind. If you want to fire up your courage, use the fear of defeat to push yourself to try harder. Turn your task into a challenge, a contest, a race. Keep your eye on the finish line and push yourself to achieve.

Courage Is
a State of Mind

*Throughout high school, my Mom always told me that
if I ever found myself compromised or scared, she
would come get me, no matter the time of day or
night. I've always told my son, now seventeen, the
same thing. Neither of us has ever called our moms.
Maybe having Mom out there gives you courage. But
probably it gives you the courage to find your own
courage.*

DAWN JOHNSTON, AGE 43

Fear is a state of mind. Courage is a state of mind. You have a choice.

Having a courageous state of mind enables you to be a leader. When you have a courageous state of mind, you're likely to give the world something to react to instead of just reacting to what the world dumps in your lap. When you're in a courageous state of mind, you're more naturally oriented toward doing what's right, in the right way, for the right reasons.

A courageous state of mind turns failures into building blocks for growth. A courageous state of mind prompts active participation. It's one thing to have courage in the face of uncontrollable situations that fill you with fear; it's another to seek opportunities that have potential for generating fear. It's the difference between being the nail and being the hammer.

In my former, corporate life, I usually worked with no fear of being fired. Most of the time, I followed my instincts, doing what

I believed was right and listening to my heart. But I fell short many times. Particularly when promotions were pending, I'd go out of my way to do the politically correct thing.

I was wrong. The way to get ahead, both in the corporate world and the real world, is to make a difference. To do that, you almost always have to turn conventional wisdom inside-out. Large corporations often have a richly deserved reputation for being conservative. But the only way to the top of the corporate structure is to be a rebel.

When a client asks me to evaluate a manager's performance, the basic question the client is posing is this: "What mark has this person left on the project?" In other words, what *wouldn't* have happened if not for this person's leadership? Or in still other words, is this a person who is willing to stick out his or her neck? Think about it. The key to success in the world's leading corporations is the same as what is seen by most of us to be the central element of failure. Corporate managers might manage. But if they aren't willing to be bold, to depart from standard operational procedures, and to have the courage to stand forth, they will never lead. Likewise, your head might be filled with dreams. But without gumption, they'll never really be real.

It's not fair. In school, we're taught to follow the rules, get in line, be quiet, and memorize the right answer. In the real world, we're rewarded for making a difference, thinking for ourselves, and challenging protocol.

In a corporate environment of reorganization and downsizing, we're usually more inclined to toe the line than lead the pack. But having consulted with executives in all manner of industries, I can tell you that the conservative follow-the-leader approach is sure death.

I've seen executives at top companies make bold decisions based on sound principles and fail spectacularly—only to be pro-

moted later. In almost every case, the promotions came because
the executives had shown themselves to be leaders with courageous mindsets—men and women who considered the facts,
weighed the risks, and took calculated chances. Sometimes they
won, sometimes they lost. But when the time came, they had the
courage to make the tough decision. Even in failure, they provided leadership and inspired their people with the passion to
make a difference.

Two years ago, I volunteered to coach a soccer team of five-
and six-year-old girls—although I'd never played the game myself. In our second season, the team made it to the championship
game. On that day, I witnessed an example of a courageous state
of mind that was at once simple and remarkable.

Both teams played to their potential. Going into the final ten
minutes of play, the score was 1–0 in our favor. It was time to
make the mandatory substitutions, required under the rules of
the league. One by one, I called out the names of the girls who'd
play out the game and assigned them to their positions. The hard
call was, who would play goalie? Normally, the girls all jumped at
the chance to play goalie. But under the circumstances, it was a
tough call. With the clock running out in the championship game
and a lead of only one goal, no one was eager to take the responsibility for preserving our lead—except for Melissa Pearce.

I turned to Melissa and asked if she felt up to playing goalie.
She told me she did, first with her eyes, then with a single word.
The look on her face was one of total determination. As she ran
onto the field pulling the goalie shirt over her head, I thought
back to the previous year, when she joined the team and played
soccer for the first time. She was petrified, avoiding the ball as if
it were a poisonous viper. But gradually, with lots of encouragement and a few successes, she gained confidence and developed
courage. There we were, leading by the slimmest of margins with

a big chunk of the game left to play in the championship game. And Melissa was the key.

My daughter, Tori, was playing defense directly in front of Melissa. Her good friend Alex was playing forward. As they took their positions, they made a pact to prevent the other team from scoring, no matter what. Those ten minutes felt like ten hours. With two minutes to go, the opposing team mounted a break to our goal. The ball was bouncing ten feet in front of our net, and three girls from the other team were poised to kick it. My heart sank. At that moment, Melissa dived head first into the fray, heedless of the three pairs of kicking feet. She got her hands on the ball and, at considerable risk to herself, put an end to the other team's chance for a score. When the clock ran out, the score was still 1–0.

Even now, when I think back to that afternoon, a shiver goes up my spine. I'll never forget seeing that little girl throw herself into that flailing frenzy of kicking feet. Melissa had entered into a state of mind that gave her the courage to do what needed to be done, despite the very real prospect that she could easily have been kicked in the head.

We had a party after the game to celebrate the season. As Melissa was leaving, I noticed she still had on the goalie shirt. Her mom told me she didn't want to take it off, saying she'd wash it and make sure it got back to me.

That wouldn't be necessary. I turned to Melissa and told her to keep the goalie shirt. She'd earned it.

Don't Make Excuses— Make Things Happen

I know of no code of honor which includes an escape clause.

WALT HARRELL

Excuses are apologies for not having courage. They're our way of making ourselves feel better about being faint of heart. They're what we use to justify our lack of action.

Making excuses is not in our best interest. Instead of being easy on ourselves, we need to be a bit curt. Drag your excuses into the harsh glare of daylight. Articulate the excuses in your head on a piece of paper. "I could never . . ."; "It's too ridiculous to even consider . . ."; "I'm not worthy . . ."; "It could never work for me . . ."

Embellish your excuses in whatever directions your imagination takes you. Build them into huge acquittals for why you didn't, haven't, can't, or wouldn't. Make fun of your excuses. Put big ears on them. Give them black eyes and broken noses. Make them look like laughingstocks. Work over your excuses until they shrivel up like the Wicked Witch of the East's legs after Dorothy landed that house on her and relieved her of those ruby slippers.

Most of the time, excuses have about that much basis in reality. They're little more than fear enablers. Recognize them for what they are and you'll take a big step toward breaking free.

Imagine if, in your career, you knew that when you tried to do your job, you'd fail two out of three times. Think of the excuses that might sprout up in your mind. Think about the ways you might justify your failures.

In Major League Baseball, a failure rate of two out of three is a huge success. A hitter who goes to the plate knows that two-thirds of the time, the crowd will boo and he'll be a bum. It's so difficult to hit a 95-mile-an-hour fastball that a batting average of .333 nearly leads the league. That's the way it is—either you accept it or you find another game to play.

Failure is part of baseball. If a hitter spent all his time making excuses for his failures, his successes would never happen. Instead of dwelling on the whiffs, a good hitter accepts them as part of the game. And dwells on the hits.

How would you react if you knew you'd be successful only a third of the time? Most of us would choke. Most of us play not to lose instead of playing to win. Or we avoid situations where there's a potential to fail, so we don't play at all. Too many of us see risks instead of opportunities. When life presents a challenge, we look for rocks to hide under when we could be using the challenge to learn, grow, and get stronger. Instead of taking action, we make excuses.

Sometimes, I wonder how some people are even able to walk. Consider how babies learn to walk. They grab on to something that looks sturdy, pull themselves up, maybe take a step, then fall. They repeat the process again and again. Then they figure out something about balance and something else about moving their feet in sequence until finally, everything comes together and they embark on legs suddenly capable of carrying them to an endless variety of new challenges.

Too often, the problem is that, while our legs are willing, our minds and hearts aren't. Instead of moving forward and risking failure, we cuddle up with our apologies. Over time, we condition ourselves to play it safe. We swallow impulses and resist the spirit of adventure, discovery, and curiosity that came naturally to us as children.

One reason so many of us avoid taking action is that we're unwilling to experience even the slightest bit of pain or discomfort. This puts us at odds with change, since change generally involves a little pain before its benefits can be realized.

So we decide that the best way is the safe way. And we think the safe way is to do nothing. But we're fooling ourselves—because not taking action is still taking an action. And we dream up excuses to protect our egos. Like "I waited too long." Or "I'd fall on my face." Or "People will laugh." Or "It's too late for me."

Excuses can be categorized under two headings—"So what?" and "Blatantly untrue." Take, for example, age—the one we use to excuse ourselves from taking up this challenge or that because we're too young or too old.

Hundreds of years ago, when the life expectancy was fifty years or so, you might have been considered old and creaky at the age of forty. Today, with life expectancy nearing eighty years, is forty still old? The truth is, age is a relative concept. Many twenty-year-olds are so set in their ways, so devoid of hope and a spirit of adventure, they might as well be put in a wheelchair equipped with a drool cup and rolled off into a corner to wait for the Grim Reaper. Contrast that with the seventy-, eighty-, and ninety-somethings who are filled with a vitality and enthusiasm that's truly inspiring.

It's never too late to try something new. Evelyn Marx is all the proof you need. She wrote her first poem a couple of years ago. Evelyn admits to being closer to ninety than she is to eighty.

But in any case, she was fairly well along in life when she wrote her first poem, fairly well along to have become as fine a poet as she is.

Age is completely beside the point to Evelyn. She talks about age as if it were a boat most people ride in, passively, as it heads faster and faster toward a huge, thundering waterfall—and at some point, they put down the oars and let whatever happens happen.

She feels sorry for people like that.

> *Not long ago, perhaps some fifty years,*
> *These frail and fractured had young love affairs.*
> *Their world has tightened, holding in its grasp*
> *these ancient children, helpless, pushed in chairs . . .*

Sometimes, Evelyn loses patience with people like that.

> *Take far away your ugly bones that,*
> *cracked and bending,*
> *now have lost their mending powers . . .*

Other times, she empathizes.

> *The nurse in white looks in and sees him dreaming.*
> *He is falling out of love with life.*
> *Don't bother him.*
> *So difficult a task, this breathing out and breathing*
> *in . . .*

And sometimes through these people, Evelyn sees into a corner of herself.

Where is the beautiful child I used to be?
With big green eyes and auburn hair.
I look in the mirror and SHE'S not me.
An old lady took my face—NOT FAIR!
The jowls below her chin—not mine.
Whose jaw is that? Whose neck? No sign
of that loveable, beautiful baby, E.

From the age of three, Evelyn has been an artist. She sold her first watercolor for $15 when she was sixteen. The wild, fanciful, howling colors of her paintings and fabricollage canvasses hang in galleries and collections all over the world.

When she turned eighty-four, her family decided she was of an age where it would be better if she sold her beachfront home and studio in Sarasota and moved to Cincinnati to be near them. So Evelyn moved into an upscale retirement community. But her new apartment was too small to accommodate her large canvasses. This discovery came, she says, "as quite a jolt." Here was a woman with a creative force that demanded an outlet on a regular basis. So shortly after she finished her most recent but perhaps not last painting, she took up poetry.

So far, Evelyn has had two books of poetry published. Not bad for such a young, only two-year-old poet. She doesn't know how her poems happen. Maybe it's because, somehow, she's still able to find the newness in things. And because she has the courage to explore.

Now that I am in Heaven, please God,
I want a room of my own.
I must be free of these smiles and nods,
This angelic friendliness.

I'm already homesick
for my blue planet, my watery home.

Time goes on. Life goes on. You really don't have much choice in the matter. No excuse is so unfair to yourself and your life journey as "I'm too old to try that."

Don't make excuses. Make things happen. Make changes. Then make history.

Legends aren't built on excuses. To my knowledge, no mourner has ever stood at the side of a grave and spoken fondly of what a wonderful legacy of excuse making the deceased left behind. The next time you find an excuse taking shape on your lips, ask yourself if it has validity or if you're simply looking for a way to justify a faintness of heart.

Use Innocence
to Your Advantage

*Courage is facing your fears even when you
have that sick feeling in the pit of your
stomach.*

TRACY DUCKWORTH, AGE 38

Have the confidence to let your lack of experience and your innocence be an advantage. Through the innocent eyes of a child, the world is forever new in every direction. Through innocent eyes, the unknown is not fearful so much as it is a thing of wonder. Through innocent eyes, dread can be transformed into anticipation. "Oh no!" can become "Oh boy!"

Occasionally, you'll look back on an experience—perhaps a dare you accepted or a risk that worked out—and you'll say, "Wow, I guess I just didn't know any better." And it was a good thing you didn't. Because if you had known better, you might not have had the courage to try. And because you didn't know any better, the experience was heightened tremendously.

It worked out that way for me on a whitewater rafting trip to the New River in West Virginia. There were seven of us in the boat, including my wife and our friends, Sandie and Brad Glass. We strapped on helmets and lifejackets and, after a half-hour course on safety, set out in our rubber raft for the first major rapids—a turbulent stretch of rock, foam, and roiling river known as "Surprise." I could hear the thunder of the rapids and see the mist rising as we approached. It looked like we were headed toward the edge of the world. Suddenly, our rubber raft was sucked into the fury.

The front of the raft went under water. Looming above us was an eight-foot wall of water. The next few seconds were a blur. But I remember Brad bouncing off me and the both of us flipping head first into the rapids. There was a moment of sheer panic. I was completely disoriented, unable to discern up from down. A moment later, I broke through the surface at the far end of the rapids. My wife, who had remained in the boat, later said she'd never seen a face as white as mine was when I broke the surface. But my panic was quickly replaced with elation. In an instant, I went from thinking "I'm going to die!" to "Hey, this is cool!" After that, I jumped off a few cliffs and, at one point, even hopped out of the raft to swim a rapid. I had fun. Brad's reaction was entirely different. He was tentative, cautious, even a bit sullen. Later at camp, I asked him what had happened. What was the big deal?

He told me about a whitewater kayaking trip he'd taken a year earlier, about how he'd flipped over going over a waterfall and nearly broken a leg. He told me stories about people going under in whitewater rafting accidents and never coming up again. The experience didn't sour Brad on whitewater rafting. But it taught him to respect the current's power.

Think about it. We both had the same experience. We both were dumped into major rapids, we both had the unsettling sensation of being disoriented and we both swallowed a quart of West Virginia river water. But there was a big difference between us. Brad knew what could happen in the rapids when you fall out of the boat. I was ignorant. As a result, our reactions to the same experience were opposites. I had a ton of fun; Brad didn't.

Which was more valuable—knowing enough to have reason to fear or not knowing anything at all? Which of us benefitted more from the experience?

All I knew about whitewater rafting was that, before I came along, lots of other people had done it and lived to talk about it. I'd known some of them, and they'd told me what a great time they'd had. I didn't know nearly as much about whitewater rafting as Brad knew.

It was a good thing I didn't. I might have missed out on a great adventure if I had.

A fine line separates innocence and ignorance from a lack of preparation. For each person and each situation, the line is different. But we often move the line too conservatively toward the end of the scale, where we insist on knowing every detail before taking action. We tend to err more on the side of holding back rather than moving forward. Too often, we're unwilling to explore because we don't know where we'll end up. It's like refusing to see a movie until you've read the script. What's the point?

A whole world of new experiences and adventures await you if you'll just move forward, even in the face of uncertainty. As a practitioner of innocence, I can vouch for the fact that your feelings of self-doubt will diminish in time. The more you push the edges of your comfort zone, the easier it gets. In this way, you can train yourself to deal with the unknown.

Your reward is the exhilaration you'll feel when you succeed. It's one thing to do something you've done a thousand times before and succeed. It's another to go where you've never gone before and snatch a victory.

Think about it. How much of a thrill do you get now from tying your own shoes, balancing on a two-wheeler, or driving a car without having your father in the seat next to you? Not much of one, right? That's because you've seen it, did it, done it.

If you're looking for real exhilaration, push the edges.

As a grown-up, when you embrace innocence, you have a politically correct excuse for failure. You can point to your own innocence as a preemptive apology for potential failure. It's all a matter of setting low expectations before you start. If that's what it takes to get going, then in this one case, I'll accept the excuse.

Innocence has insulated me from the fear of the unknown. When my first daughter was born, I was blissfully unaware of all the problems that could arise. My wife, who is a registered nurse and who had years of experience working on maternity wards, was not.

She had a reaction to the epidural that caused her blood pressure to drop sharply. I knew something had happened because the alarm on the monitor sounded and the nurses and doctors were responding quickly, but I didn't know to what. In my innocence, I assumed all was well when the monitor began beeping normally again. Fortunately, as it turned out for me, I was unable to understand all the technospeak that was going on between my wife and the nurses and doctors.

When Kristyn emerged, I beamed just as any new father would. But my innocence quickly abated as I received a quick education in the birthing process.

Kristyn's lungs were suctioned, and she was rushed from the delivery room to intensive care. When Debbie's blood pressure had dropped, the decreased flow of blood to the baby had caused her to breathe in contaminated amniotic fluid. For the first week of her life, Kristyn lay in intensive care under an oxygen hood with intravenous antibiotics.

She's fine now. And Debbie and I have added two more children to our family. But I'm no longer an innocent, beaming dad. With my newfound knowledge of everything that can go wrong, each beep of the monitor during the births of Tori and Brad sent me into arrhythmia. Neither had anything remotely like the traumatic experience Kristyn had. But both presented numerous opportunities to learn about other unpleasant, everyday childhood maladies, providing me with more of an education on subjects than I really ever wanted.

So if you're feeling a little out of the loop, consider it a positive. If you knew everything that could go wrong, you might never do anything.

Be like a child. Consider the advantages. A child approaches even the smallest, most humdrum aspect of life as an adventure, making no pretense of knowledge or experience. The child's world is defined by discovery, imagination, and growth. He's encouraged to approach new experiences with an open mind—to try new vegetables, to haul himself up on his hind legs and take that first step, to meet new people, to try trumpet lessons.

Granted, knowledge is power. A little knowledge is valuable, no doubt. At the same time, it can fill you with unfounded fears. And too many unfounded fears can paralyze you. Don't be afraid of innocence. But don't settle into it, either. Temper your hunger for knowledge with a spirit of adventure. Use innocence to fuel your curiosity. Think of innocence as the doorway to discovery, wonder, and adventure.

The Power of
Quiet Confidence

---

*How much courage some people display in a
given situation depends on who, if anyone, is
watching.*

WALT HARRELL

Courage comes from believing in the external value of your task. It also comes from having an internal belief in who you are and what you can do.

It helps to like yourself. Not "like" in the New Age sensitive I'm-a-worthy-person kind of self-liking. "Like" in the sense of respecting yourself for who you are, for what you've done in the past and the belief that the values you hold are true and proper. "Like" in the sense that, whatever happens, you see yourself as a person whose instinct won't be to take the course of least resistance, but who will do the right things in the right way.

At its best, liking oneself manifests itself in quiet confidence. If you truly like yourself, you're at peace with yourself. Quiet confidence requires an exceptional sense of self-mastery. Most people can sense quiet confidence immediately, because it's relatively rare. It doesn't rely on flash, hype, smugness, or arrogance to communicate itself. When you have quiet confidence, you have no need to be defensive or offensive.

Your life may have many different journeys, some that overlap and others that are distinct from all the rest. For example, a man can be a husband, worker, father, artist, handyman, and member of the community. In any case, your confidence varies from one journey to the next. In some areas, you may feel secure to the level of having quiet confidence. In others, your lack of confidence can leave you feeling naked to the world.

When you consider your various life journeys and how much confidence you have in respect to each one, you'll begin to understand the areas where you need to make adjustments. Like tires on a car, you need to balance your various journeys to find fulfillment.

In the early years of Richard Saunders International, when Richard Saunders International was just Jack Gordon and myself working in my basement, we had a standing joke. Whenever a client had a request, no matter how huge or unreasonable, the answer was always, "No problem." In our minds, we were invincible. We could accomplish anything. And somehow, we usually did.

It wasn't a marketing pitch. It was our way of creating a veneer of confidence—no matter how thin—in what we could do for our clients. The truth was, we often had no idea what we were getting into—but we were always willing to sail the company into uncharted waters. We were always willing to embark on new missions.

Sometimes, the willingness to try anything resulted in flaming crashes. More often, it opened doors. Today, I have a solid foundation of people, processes, and skills capable of delivering high quality ideas in a hurry. I'm slowly but surely building a sense of quiet confidence in my company's abilities—and in my own.

It's a continuing process. If there's one lesson I've learned, it's that it's easier to be quietly confident when everything is going smoothly. The challenge is in maintaining the confidence to stay the course when the seams are unraveling.

Quiet confidence is contagious. When one person demonstrates it—whether it's a matter of standing up for what's right or exposing oneself to risk for a good cause—others pick up on it. It inspires courage in them as well. And their courage comes back in turn to reinforce the first person.

Jason Bell is that sort of person. At the age of sixteen, when his life was scraping bottom, he displayed a quiet confidence that was truly inspiring to those around him.

Jason had leukemia. He thought of it as "a major bummer." An intravenous catheter had been implanted in his chest, into the vein leading into his heart. Two rounds of chemotherapy were begun. Jason's father, Jim, remembered a conversation they had one night early on when Jason was having trouble falling asleep: "He said, 'Dad, I've been thinking about how life can pass you by.' He didn't know what was going to happen, and he was afraid. I don't think he has lost the fear. But somewhere along the line, he made the decision not to let the fear control him."

Jason's doctors had a long list of things they didn't want him to do. No swimming, no heavy lifting, no soccer. "Soccer is important to me," Jason said. "Without it, I wouldn't feel whole. So much had become abnormal in my life, I wanted to be like a normal kid." Jason was insistent. His dad considered the alternatives. The worst that could happen would be, somebody might accidentally grab the catheter that extended six inches from Jason's chest and yank it out. There'd be a mad dash to the hospital. Jason would lose a lot of blood. On the other hand, soccer could do more for Jason than medicine. It would help him be normal.

Jason's stepmother, Jan, showed up at the first practice in August to explain a few things to the coach and the boys on the team. Like about Jason's IV connector. Like how, if he should get hit in the chest and start bleeding, the coach should stick his finger in the hole to stop the flow and get somebody to dial 911. Basic stuff like that.

Jason's quiet confidence helped his coach, Ken Stoll, forget his own fear: "Jason could barely keep up in one lap around the field at the first few practices. But as the year went on, I forgot about his leukemia. The other players forgot about it, too. We all stopped thinking of him as being sick or having any kind of disability."

It turned out to be an exasperating 1–14–1 season for the Mariemont Warriors. It was what coaches call "a rebuilding year." Of the nineteen players on the roster, fourteen were freshmen and sophomores. The Warriors' only victory was the season opener. Jason scored two assists. But in a larger sense, the season was a glittering triumph. Especially for Jason. "I wasn't counting on him for much that first game," Jason's coach said. "But he got stronger and stronger each week. By the end of the season, I was counting on him heavily."

Ken Stoll has been coaching soccer for twenty years now. Of all the players on all his teams, there are a handful he'll never forget. Mostly, they were all-stars—kids who made the team look good with their talent. The thing Coach Stoll will never forget about Jason was his quiet confidence. "Here was this small, slender kid—a kid with leukemia—absolutely going for it," Stoll said. "When things get tough, I think about Jason Bell."

Your confidence in your values and abilities undergo their most rigorous tests in the face of failure. These are the loneliest of times; times when you feel your fears tearing at you from all sides; times when the temptation to give up is strong.

These are the times to remember your mission—and to ask yourself these questions: Am I doing the right thing? Am I doing it for the right reasons? Do I believe in my mission? Is it worth the price I'll have to pay?

Take your time. Talk it over with someone you respect. Be honest. If the answers to those questions are yes, and if you're confident in your cause, you'll realize your mission is pure. And in that realization, you'll find the quiet confidence you need to take the next step.

Take Action—
Do It Now

When I'm eighty I want to look at myself in the mirror and say I did it right. And the only way to do that is to look at myself in the mirror today and say I'm doing it right.

MICHELLE MARTIN, AGE 23

It usually doesn't matter what action you take in the face of fear, as long as you take some action. That's how it is with fear. If you take action—pretty much any action at all—you increase your chances of defeating the beast. It's simple. Do something, and something will happen. Do nothing, and nothing will happen. When you take a step forward, you'll find new courage.

Trying something new is like peering over the next ridge of mountains. With each new experience, you gain new insights, which you can use like a weapon against fear. By taking action, you learn about your fears. And as you learn about your fears, you gain control over them. Of course, this requires huge amounts of energy. Of course, you have to work hard at it. In fact, you have to do the best you can.

Fear shrinks dramatically when you know you're doing the best you can. Putting forth your best effort is liberating. Consider the times in your life when you've failed at something knowing you've given it your best effort. Then think about times you fell short because the effort you brought to a task wasn't what it should have been. Which experiences did the least amount of damage to your self-respect?

By taking action, you're taking matters into your own hands, as opposed to leaving them to chance. You exert yourself and, in so doing, you use your fear to fight fear. This is the essence of courage.

The most effective system I know of for tracking your tangible action against your priorities is "The Action Priorities Audit." It's based on this principle: where your body is, your heart and mind cannot be far behind. If you spend most of your time at the dining room table helping your child with math homework, your child's math skills are what's most important to you. If you're on the golf course all the time, your swing is what matters most to you. If you're always meeting with prospective customers, your priorities are set on sales.

Make a list of the ways you've spent your time over the past week and how much time you've spent doing what. Focus on where your physical being was and what you were doing. You can base it on a twenty-four–hour schedule or you can zero in on the time that's variable, when you have flexibility. An audit for a week usually gives you a clear reading of the priorities that are getting your true effort. Break it down to hours and minutes or half-day increments. Precision is not as important as orders of magnitude.

If your priority challenge is in your job, track your work schedule. If you own a business, you might track how much time you've spent selling, managing, training, developing new products, and performing administrative tasks. If your priority challenge is in your personal life, you might track how much time you spend with your spouse or each of your children—or reading, learning, exercising, or pursuing hobbies. Compare where your body was over the period of your audit as opposed to where you wished it had been. On a sheet of paper, list the various ways you spent your time and figure the percent of your total time you devoted to each category. Now make a second column and list your ideal percentages.

PRIORITIES AUDIT FOR PERSONAL TIME	CURRENT %	IDEAL %
Time spent with children		
Time spent on exercise		
Time spent with spouse		
Time spent learning or studying		
Time spent on hobbies		
Total		

Seeing how you spend your time in black and white is the first step toward rearranging your priorities for the better. It also helps you take action on them.

The impact of refocusing your energies against priority objectives can be immense. I learned this lesson working in corporate America. After a frustrating year of trying to create new products, I resolved to eliminate all activities that didn't make a direct contribution to results. For a full year, I made a conscious effort to focus 90 percent of my time on productive efforts, which led me to a decision to declare a personal embargo on any meetings that didn't involve decision making or tangible product development. I also discontinued all nonproductive paperwork and all other bureaucratic bodily functions. As a result, I set a company record for bringing nine business initiatives to market in the ensuing 12 months.

*   *   *

When I think about taking action, I think of Then Vin.

Then—he pronounces it "Ten"—was a senior at a largely white, largely middle-class high school when his story appeared in the *Cincinnati Post*. At the time, he was making plans for college. He wasn't quite sure what he wanted to be, but he wasn't asking for much—just a chance at a future with a little security.

Then was born in Cambodia, in a town called Battambang, where there was no such thing as a secure future. He told an amazing story that is impossible to corroborate. But to Then, such stories were routine among the Cambodian refugees who survived the Khmer Rouge in the mid-1970s.

This is his story, as he told it:

"I was six years old when the Khmer Rouge took me from my family and put me in a concentration camp for boys. I saw many horrible things—people beaten to death, shot, tortured. You had to make yourself very small so they wouldn't notice you. They made us work in the rice paddy, clear the forests, build roads. It was dark when they got us out of bed and dark when we quit work. They fed us one meal a day—a bowl of water and a little rice. At night, we would eat rats, snakes, grasshoppers, anything we could find. You would be surprised at what you will do to survive."

He lost track of time, of sunrises and sunsets. He focused only on his fear and on taking whatever action was required to stay alive—until one day, he found himself facing a decision. He could give in to circumstances and wait for the end. Or he could take action—and take his chances in the jungle.

"After a while, I was too sick to work anymore," he said. "I knew I would be shot, so I took my risks. I knew if I could go anyplace and stay alive, it would have to be in the jungle. Because no one would follow me. It is too dangerous. So I ran away. I didn't have anything. Only a pair of black shorts."

Imagine yourself in that situation. Imagine taking that kind of action.

"I slept in the trees, way up," he said. "I became like a monkey, going from tree to tree without touching the ground. I stayed close to the trees because of the wild boars. I ate all the fruit I could find. Mushrooms, too. I ate a poison one once and was very sick, maybe for two weeks. But I learned. And as time passed, I knew I would live."

The jungle was the backdrop for a second Khmer Rouge camp where Then's father was imprisoned, working in a paddy to raise rice to feed the other prisoners. Again, Then took action. He sneaked in one night. "My father got me a slingshot and a dagger. I went back to the jungle and used them to kill birds. I had plenty of food after that. I don't know how long it was. But when the North Vietnamese drove the Khmer Rouge from Cambodia, the prisoners were released. My father came into the jungle to find me. That's how I learned the war was over."

Then told of being reunited with his parents, spending several years in a refugee camp in Thailand. Once more, he took action and stepped into an entirely different kind of jungle—in 1983, he came to America. He learned English as an eighth grader at With-row High School in Cincinnati. When his family moved to Atlanta a year later, he wanted to stay. His language teacher, Pat Friedmann, invited him to live with her family.

Years later, Then was still having nightmares of soldiers chasing him. But they were gradually becoming less frequent, less vivid. And his concerns were no longer of the life-and-death variety. He was worried more about making the honor roll.

Still, he had a 3.45 grade-point average, achieved largely in accelerated courses. Princeton University had been talking to him. That was his dream, to go to Princeton. The hard part would be deciding on a career. Maybe, he said, he would become an engineer. Or maybe would go into forestry; he loves being in the wilderness. He wasn't sure. All he knew was that, when the time came, he would take action.

In my career, I have been blessed with copious amounts of publicity, built largely on self-initiated publicity stunts—or for the more squeamish among you, "positive public relations exposure."

There's nothing particularly mysterious about getting media attention. It's quite simple. It's all about taking action. If you create news, reporters will write about it. The key is, you can't wait to be discovered. You have to make a spark to light the fire. You have to take action to get a reaction.

Amazingly enough, if you don't do anything fairly far removed from the ordinary, you don't get publicity. From long before the days of P. T. Barnum, publicity has been focused on people who take action and dare to do the unusual. Think about it. When was the last time you saw a front-page headline about an everyday man or woman fulfilling an everyday obligation or otherwise engaged in an everyday activity?

In my business, publicity makes all the difference between prosperity and withering on the vine. Here are some of the stunts I staged, either on my own or with my team, to generate national exposure. Each case required necks to be stuck out. Each required us to take action, and each triggered valuable results:

- At Procter & Gamble, I was challenged to create interest in Spic & Span. An old brand, for years it had been quietly fulfilling its everyday obligation to clean floors, and consequently, sales were stagnant. I took action to put sparkle into a Valentine's Day promotion. Inside every bottle, the company put either a genuine one-third carat diamond or a cubic zirconium of equal size. The event generated millions of dollars' worth of exposure and the first surge in sales in more than a decade.

- One holiday season, I introduced two board games to America. To stir the media pot, I took action and assembled a press packet announcing a new company called HaHa!, with a card proclaiming myself King of the Elves and a goofy photograph of myself dressed in forest-green tights and shoes with pointy, curled-up toes. *Entertainment Tonight* and other media outlets gave it a run that paid dividends long after. It never would have happened if I'd waited for the phone to ring.

- Once I was looking for a way to publicize the Eureka! Mansion. I took action and hired a "nationally known and respected psychic" to help me "contact" Elvis Presley, Ben Franklin, and any spirits that might have been inhabiting the mansion. We never hooked up with the King, but the *Wall Street Journal* reported that "Benjamin Franklin was in the air." The promotion resulted in a great story in the *Journal*, along with an informative profile of my company.

- Sometimes you don't take action so much as you react to a circumstance in a way to turn it to your favor. One day, I got a call from Andy Wolf, one of Morley Safer's producers for *60 Minutes*. He'd read about us in various publications, including the *Wall Street Journal*, and wanted to learn more about Richard Saunders International.

I invited him for a visit. You don't say no to *60 Minutes*, especially if you're a kid from Maine who doesn't know any better. Andy was advised to bring an extra set of clothing and a sense of humor. On the morning of his arrival, I convened my team. A red carpet was rolled down the front walkway. My allies hid in strategic positions at the second-floor windows and around the corner of the building. As Andy came up the front walk, I stepped out the door to greet him. When he hit the red carpet, dozens of water balloons came raining down from the second floor. Jack Gordon baptized our visitor with a water cannon. In a neat twist of irony, the episode was recorded on a hidden video camera.

That's the story of how we ambushed *60 Minutes*. Yes, I was a little apprehensive about the fallout. But my thinking was that if Andy went back to New York in a snit, I'd have had a valuable story about what it takes to get *60 Minutes* off your back. As it was, Andy was a sport. He never produced a story about my company for *60 Minutes*, because none of my clients was willing to give him the total freedom he required—and *60 Minutes* doesn't exactly have a reputation for treating businesses gently. Nevertheless, it was an action that paid off: word of the *60 Minutes* hose-down spread and eventually, the Richard Saunders International crew was featured on *Dateline NBC*—not once, but twice in two years.

• The most outrageous publicity stunt I ever attempted was "The Planet Eureka! Budget Deficit Tour," assigned to come up with ideas to solve a problem that has Congress stymied—the federal budget deficit. Working through the office of Congressman John Kasich, the U.S. House of Representatives' budget chairman, my team convened a Eureka! session with congressional staffers—complete with the usual regimen of Nerf guns, Silly String, and high volume rock 'n' roll. After similar idea generating sessions at Harvard University and with union labor leaders at the Eureka! Mansion, we culled the best from a mountain of ideas and tested them with registered voters through AcuPOLL.

The results were presented to Congressman Kasich in a press conference on Capitol Hill. More than three dozen news organizations attended. Not only did we garner considerable ink and air time, the action we took actually had an impact on the deficit, judging by a letter from Congressman Kasich: "Basic principles developed by your Planet Eureka! inventors have held firm throughout the budget process." He referred to our effort in a follow-up letter as "a genuine national service." I'd like to think my forefather, Lyman Hall, whose name appears among the signers of the Declaration of Independence, would have been proud.

Altogether, these events generated roughly $20 million of, for the most part, free publicity, catapulting Richard Saunders International from a dream in my basement to a leader in its field. The point is, none of it would have happened if I hadn't taken action. Collectively, the events defined my company to the world. If I'd sat waiting for the word to get out, the word wouldn't have budged. And the vast majority of my clients would never have heard of Richard Saunders International.

How does this translate to your life? Like this: Unless you take action, you'll never get anywhere other than where you are at this moment. You're probably not thinking about launching an international consulting firm. But I bet you're facing one or two challenges or more that would become a whole lot less vague if you took action on them. What are you waiting for? Get going. Try something, anything. Only by doing something different can you cause something different to occur.

Think about it. What tangible actions can you take? How can you increase your odds by increasing the number of attempts you make? If you increase your actions by tenfold, what might you achieve? Are you afraid of taking too big a step? What small steps could you take to build your confidence?

Do something, anything. Move your feet and your body will follow. Don't sit back and let life happen to you. Participate in it. Take action. Do it now.

Declare Your Intentions
Before Entering the Arena

Courage is hard to recognize at the time because the dark clouds are looming. You're scared because there's no right answer. And yet you keep wondering "but what if . . . ?" In the end, only you can decide if your life is worth living to the fullest . . . but it takes courage.

ROSEANN HASSEY, AGE 34

I n the heat of battle, it's hard to draw a bead on your target. It's difficult halfway through the journey to maintain your courage when you're distracted by one obstacle after another.

You need bulletproof encouragement. You can have it if you determine what your limits are before you enter the fray. Know what your range is against the backdrop of your goals before you draw your sword.

When I was a sophomore at the University of Maine, I decided to follow in my father's footsteps. As a U of M undergraduate, he sold advertising space on desktop blotters to local businesses. By the time I arrived on campus, someone else was selling blotters. So I took what I thought was the next best advertising medium — vinyl telephone book covers.

My intentions were clear and simple. Over Christmas break, I declared my intentions:

- WHEN: I would engage in selling advertising space on vinyl telephone book covers for one week commencing January 15.
- WHO: I would target those businesses that catered especially to college students. These included Pat's Pizza, purveyor of the world's most delectable pizza; Governor's Restaurant, home of the most succulent burgers east of the Penobscot River; and the Oronoka Restaurant, the only restaurant I know of that gives away free steamed clams after 10 P.M. every Wednesday.
- WHAT: I would sell one-inch ads for $60 apiece. Should I find it necessary to discount, I would go no lower than $40 per ad.

So far, so good. On the ride back to campus in my silver '72 Dodge Coronet, a magnificent vehicle equipped with eight gaping cylinders of gas-guzzling mechanized power, my thoughts were occupied with the many ways I would indulge myself with the revenue from all the advertising space I was about to sell.

The University of Maine is located in the town of Orono, just north of Bangor. January in that neck of America is cold and ugly—the sort of conditions that make door-to-door salesmanship a job for either the truly courageous or the truly stupid. Most of all, it requires a good set of warm clothes. Looking back, I don't recall the thermometer ever climbing above zero until March that year.

On the designated day, I set out at eight o'clock in the morning with my pitch and my plan of attack. I was a little scared by that time, and not just of frostbite. I'd never before sold anything so abstract as advertising space. My courage shriveled when the first two businessmen I approached recoiled in shock at the thought of having their establishments named on vinyl phone book covers. They explained that, five years earlier, some slicker swept through town selling ads and collecting deposits before disappearing entirely, never to be seen in the greater metropolitan Orono area again.

But I kept plugging. It began snowing and, in minutes, I was walking from door to door with an inch of snow on my shoulders. I was beginning to lose sensation in my feet, having stepped off a curb onto a layer of ice that was too thin to support my weight but thick enough to give the appearance of solid pavement, filling my shoes with frigid slush.

By 10 A.M., I had zero sales.

By eleven, I hadn't done any better.

By noon, it was the same story.

Finally, at one o'clock, a dear, sweet woman at the Orono Savings and Loan bought a one-inch, one-column ad for $60. I set forth with renewed vigor, forsaking lunch to hit Orono's major business concerns. To my shock and dismay, I was turned down flat by the key companies on my sure-thing list: Pat's Pizza, Governor's Restaurant, and the Oronoka.

Once again, my confidence was ebbing, especially after a door was literally slammed in my face—and on my foot. The person on the other side of the door graciously kicked my wounded appendage free from the jamb. It was at that point that I learned there's something worse than having feet that are merely cold and wet.

By 4:45 P.M., I was seriously dismayed. I'd burned up more than eight hours covering what I thought were hot prospects and had a measly $60 to show for it. Meanwhile, my vaunted vinyl telephone-book covers were going to cost $600 to produce. I felt chewed up in the jagged jaws of failure.

Climbing behind the cracked dash of the Coronet, I headed back to the dorm. There on the seat beside me was another intention I'd declared but forgotten. The evening before, I'd scrawled out one last intention:

SELL UNTIL 5 P.M.—DON'T GIVE UP!!!

It had seemed like the right thing the night before—back when I didn't have frozen, bruised feet and a masticated ego.

But a deal's a deal. I'd declared my intentions, and I had to stick with them. Besides, I had only fifteen minutes to go.

I made a what-the-heck call on Residential Life, the organization that ran the dormitories. Summoning up what was left of my courage, I asked to see the vice president of student living. To my surprise, I was ushered immediately into the vice president's office—probably because there weren't many people out on a day like that and he wanted some company.

It was five o'clock. I launched into my best pitch. I figured if I was going to go down in flames, I would go down with every bit of energy still flickering in my body. Somehow, something clicked. The vice president of student living pointed to the bottom of my sample cover. "How much would that be?" he asked. My jaw dropped. I picked up my jaw and asked, uh, er, what exactly was he looking for in terms of space? He told me he was interesting in the bottom half of the front page. I did a quick calculation and arrived at a figure. Nine hundred dollars. It was all I could do to keep my voice from cracking. No—that's not quite true. It was all I could to keep from dropping to my knees and kissing his cordovans.

The vice president of student living said my price seemed fair enough. Then he asked me if I was all right. I explained that, oh yeah, sure, I was fine. Yeah, it was a bit nippy outside and I had a bad foot. But I'd make it. He expressed his sympathy and called in his secretary to make out a purchase order.

When I floated out of his office at twenty after five, my new business, Campus Promotions International, was off and running. I had renewed confidence, which translated to renewed energy. In the following week, I sold more than $2,000 in additional advertisements. Looking back, I don't think I really believed in my vinyl phone-book covers as an advertising vehicle—and it showed in my presentation. But with that first big sale, I found the confidence and courage to brave the chilliest windchill factors. More importantly, if I hadn't decided in advance, outside of the field of play, to persevere until five o'clock, I never would've succeeded. Granted, I had a lucky break, scoring a big sale on that last call. But when you work hard—and you keep up the effort, despite the discomfort of the moment, as considerable as it may be—good things have a way of happening. It's all a matter of If. When you don't shy away from If, luck has a way of turning from bad to good. No matter how sore your feet might be.

Mapping out a plan of attack and sticking to it, come what may, is sometimes the best way to encourage courage—especially when you're running up against hurdles in the early going. In times like that, when you're taking the first small steps toward your goal, long before you've built momentum, discipline can be the difference between success and failure.

When you declare your intentions, you make a promise. Sometimes, it's a promise to yourself. Other times, it's a promise to someone else. When Alberto Jose Morales declared his intentions, he made a promise to the woman he loved.

A photograph reminds him of his promise. His bride was looking into the camera, her eyes clear and confident. He wore the slightly dazed expression of a young man deeply in love. In sickness and in health, they anticipated their future.

Forty-six years later, the photo is tacked to the wall behind the counter at Al's small Spanish restaurant, The Madrid. He's sixty-five, old enough to retire. But he has obligations to meet, an ailing wife to look after and intentions he declared long ago that he intends to fulfill.

Her name is Beryl. She was working for the Royal Air Force as an accountant. He was with the U.S. Army Air Corps. They met in an air-raid shelter.

"The shelter was blacked out," he says. "I couldn't see her, she couldn't see me. But I knew she was there, and I struck up a conversation. When the bombing stopped and the lights came on, I saw her for the first time. She was a beauty—auburn hair, gorgeous smile. I told myself, 'Al, this is the girl you're going to marry.'"

It was a promise he made himself. She carried red roses at the wedding, on the day they declared their intentions publicly. Other more recent photos are on the wall behind the counter, too. One taken at a costume party at the hospital shows Al and Beryl in fake noses and glasses. In another, Al is holding a great-grandson and grinning at the camera. Beryl's eyes have faded. A strap holds her head against the back of the wheelchair.

Beryl has Parkinson's disease. Al took care of her for eleven years. Six years ago, he moved her into the hospital. "Since them, she's lost her speech," Al says. "Most of her sight and movement, too. But she can hear. I can look at her face and tell if she's in pain, if she's laughing, if she's frightened or happy or sad. I see her every evening. I tell her how my day went. Or I read to her or play a tape of English folk music. She'd do the same for me."

It's been a good marriage. Always has, always will be. In sickness and in health, Al's keeping a promise he made forty-six years ago.

*   *   *

Never ever give up is more than a political slogan—it's a call to personal responsibility. Success requires perseverance. When you persevere, the victory is that much sweeter. When you persevere and win, you gain confidence and satisfaction that reverberates long after the challenge has been met. Hard-won victories pay dividends for years to come.

Look at your life. What promises did you make yourself when you were younger? What New Year's resolutions have you made? What vows have you made to your parents, spouse, children, friends? Which have you kept? Which have you let slide? What can you do now to reconcile them?

Multiply Your Risks, Divide Your Fears

Courage cannot exist without risk . . . these are two words that a thesaurus should list side by side.

TINA MIMS, AGE 37

Manage your fears. Put them in a portfolio and treat them as if they were financial investments.

It's a classic rule of financial management: don't sink all your money into a single investment. Scan the horizon. Find out what's out there. Look into a diverse range of possibilities, then invest in a variety of the brightest options you can find. That's the way to increase your odds. That's the smart thing.

The same principle plugs nicely into other corners of life. Say you need more money. You look at your options. Off the top of your head, you decide you can rob a convenience store, work toward a raise or try to find another job. You skip the first option because of legal ramifications. The other two seem to make more sense, so you pursue them. By combining your efforts, you've reduced your fear of taking meaningful action in either direction. On the other hand, consider what often happens when you act in a linear fashion, limiting your efforts to one pursuit at a time. You might spend months building your case for a raise, only to be told no.

Successful entrepreneurs are adept at hedging their bets. Few are actually risk takers. Most of the time, they have a "back door" solution for every contingency. When I launched my business, I reduced my risks—and therefore, my fears—through a kind of portfolio risk management. Instead of starting a single business, I started three—each with a synergistic link to the other, but each with the potential to stand on its own.

The first, Richard Saunders International, was designed to invent and articulate new products and services. The second, AcuPOLL Research, was developed to gauge the likelihood of Richard Saunders's new product and service concepts succeeding in the marketplace. The third, the Eureka! Institute, offered creativity training, based on the techniques we used to develop ideas at Richard Saunders.

The first two endeavors turned quick profits. The third made money, but at a much slower pace. In the process, I learned something about my own interests. I found myself drawn more to the creativity side of my business then the research and creativity training facets. When the opportunity came, I sold AcuPOLL to concentrate on my first love. Meanwhile, the Eureka! Institute focused increasingly on writing books and less on lecturing. And Richard Saunders International grew in proportion to the attention I was able to devote to it.

Overall, I minimized the risk of launching a new business by launching three businesses simultaneously. As I developed a sense of what the market wanted—and how I wanted to spend my time— I was better able to focus on the best of the three options. And as my risks and fears were divided, my confidence was increased.

Diversity isn't defined by minor variations on a theme. It's a matter of doing that which is dramatically different. Sometimes, multiplying your risks requires you to step out of character, hold your breath and take the long shot. It also requires you to give chaos elbow room. When you diversify, especially in the beginning, you're engaged in a delicate, difficult balancing act, one that can be physically and mentally exhausting.

In the early days of my business, I toiled for what seemed like twenty-seven hours a day. Neither you nor I can keep up that kind of pace very long. But you can do it for a while. If you should ever find yourself taking this path, I suggest you give yourself a defined period of time. Decide at the outset to stop, look around you after six, twelve, or eighteen months and cut loose those pursuits at which you aren't making discernible progress.

To ease the energy drain of diversifying, look for opportunities with potential for synergy. In my case, developing a lecture helped define my beliefs and principles, leading to increased effectiveness in my consulting efforts, which in turn help me form solid hypotheses for my research company.

How can you put the power of diversity to work in your own life? Here are a few possibilities:

- Instead of sending out a handful of resumes and making a handful of follow-up calls, drop 100 resumes in the mail.
- Instead of taking one car for a test drive because you like the way it looks, check out an entire squadron. That way, you won't get stuck making payments on a ride you find isn't right for you.
- Instead of working one entry level job, work two on different shifts until you have enough experience to make an informed decision as to which offers the best opportunity for growth.
- Instead of preparing a single new recipe the night of a dinner party, try three recipes a week ahead of time. Pick the best of this and the best of that.

One year, I mailed Thanksgiving cards to clients. The card included a photo of myself dressed as Ben Franklin—in keeping with the fact that my company's name was inspired by Franklin's pen name, Richard Saunders, the name he used to write *Poor Richard's Almanac*. The card was accompanied with a recipe for white turkey chili, in honor of Franklin's suggestion that the turkey, not the bald eagle, should be the national bird of the United States.

> *The Bald Eagle is a Bird of bad moral Character; he does not get his living honestly. Besides, he is a rank Coward; the little kingbird, not bigger than a Sparrow, attacks him boldly and drives the Eagle away.*
>
> *In truth the Turk'y is a much more respectable Bird, a true original Native of America. The Turk'y is a little vain and silly, it is true, but not the worse emblem for that. The Turk'y is a Bird of Courage, and would not hesitate to attack a Grenadier of the British Guards, who should presume to invade his FarmYard with a red coat on.*
>
> Ben Franklin
> letter from Paris,
> 1784

I used the concept of portfolio risk management to develop the turkey chili recipe. First, I made a double batch of the base mix of beans and chopped turkey. Then I divided the mixture into four pans, giving each a dose of something different. Into one, I poured a beer. Into another, I ladled salad dressing. Into a another, I dumped hot sauce.

With no small fanfare, I presented four bowls of chili each to my wife and my sister, Pam. The beer recipe was a winner. A couple of others ended up in the garbage disposal.

I later learned that turkey leftovers from Thanksgiving dinners from across America were used to make my chili. A lot of clients said they liked it a lot. Portfolio risk management made the recipe happen quickly and efficiently. For your culinary consideration, it's reprinted below.

••••••

POOR RICHARD'S "WICKED GOOD" WHITE TURKEY CHILI

2 tablespoons olive oil

1 medium onion, well chopped

¼ teaspoon garlic powder or 2 large garlic cloves

½ tablespoon oregano

1 12-ounce beer

2 16-ounce cans great northern white beans (drained and
    rinsed)

1 pound leftover cooked diced turkey meat (or chicken
    breasts)

6 ounces shredded white cheddar cheese

Creative Miscellanea: hot sauce, sour cream, salt, pepper,
    salsa, cilantro, bacon bits

1. Sauté onions, garlic and oregano with olive oil in deep skillet or chili pot for 5 minutes.
2. Add beans and beer and bring to a boil.
3. Reduce heat and simmer for 30 minutes.
4. Add turkey and cheese and cook till blended.
5. Add your own Creative Miscellanea to taste

••••••

The key to portfolio risk management is to latch onto as many options you can think of, then keep them open as long as you can before signing on the dotted line. Keep your options open so that when the right situation presents itself, you're ready to move.

To get along as a portfolio risk manager, you have to be willing to accept failure. Failure is built into the system. Indeed, it's one of its great advantages. With this approach, you're more willing to take on more novel, more new-and-different risks because you have a safety net; the knowledge you have other options. Alternatively, when you put all your efforts in a single, concerted effort, the natural inclination is to make decisions fraught with compromise, which is only a short distance from mediocrity.

Think about it. Do you insist on a single right answer or are you willing to risk a little chaos that goes with juggling a variety of options? Do you search for alternatives or do you suffer from tunnel vision? Are you comfortable with short-term failures or do a few small failures in the pursuit of a larger goal keep you from persevering?

Most of all, are you bored? The chaos that occurs when you're dealing with all the diverse elements or a risk portfolio will solve that problem for you in a hurry!

When Everyone Else Admires the Emperor's New Clothes

Character is not joining in when you're on the playground and all your friends are picking on the fat kid. Courage is walking over to shoot hoops with the fat kid.

MIKE KATZ, AGE 37

Pity the poor, deluded emperor. He was such a clothes horse, that, when two strangers offered to make a new outfit for his birthday from a bolt of magic cloth, he jumped at it. The cool thing about the magic cloth, the strangers told the emperor, was that only the enlightened would be able to see it. To the ignorant, unwise or otherwise doltish, the cloth would be invisible.

Hey, no problem, the emperor said—all the time thinking a suit made from magic cloth could help him ferret out those of his advisors and counselors who weren't worth their castle keep.

It's the ultimate fable of political correctness. When the emperor first saw the alleged cloth, he suppressed a gasp. He couldn't see it. But he didn't mention it for fear of showing his own lack of discernment. And everyone in the castle followed suit, so to speak.

As the emperor walked through the streets in his new birthday suit, no one said a word. Until one child hollered, "Hey, wait a minute—the emperor has no clothes!" A murmur skittered through the crowd as, one by one, the emperor's subjects were compelled to agree. But the emperor continued the charade, despite his goosebumps, too proud to admit his failing.

When established authorities, like an emperor's court, issue a royal decree, it's easy to be swept up in the charade. And once the tide of conventional wisdom sweeps through the countryside, it takes strength to stand in opposition. It's so much less complicated to blend in with the crowd.

Unfortunately, conventional wisdom often isn't so wise. Experts are often mistaken. What the masses believe to be right is sometimes based more on precedent than fact.

My four-year-old son, Brad, might have a better idea than the rest of society about the proper way to wear socks. The conventional wisdom is that socks should match. But since he was old enough to pick his own socks from the sock drawer, Brad has picked socks of different colors. Instead of two white or two blue socks, he prefers to wear one that's blue and one that's white. He wears socks that match his shirt and pants—one matches his shirt, the other matches his pants.

Brad's family has come to accept his taste in hosiery. Whenever some well-intentioned person outside the family mentions to him that his socks are mismatched, he begs to differ. Look, he says—this sock matches my pants and this sock matches my shirt.

The boy is willing to stand apart. He has a good point. He's got a good idea, too. Different colors of socks are more interesting to look at and much easier to find in a sock drawer. I wonder how long he'll maintain his sock independence in a world of footwear conformity.

When you get the feeling in the pit of your stomach that the crowd is going the wrong way, it can eat away at you. Sometimes, the feeling won't go away—no matter how fervently you wish it would. It's hard to subject yourself to the potential ridicule and isolation that happens when you stand alone. Humans are fundamentally social creatures. We like to be liked. By going against the grain, you risk becoming outcast, friendless and abandoned. To get along, we're taught to go along. We're taught that conformity is the way to gain community acceptance.

But the easy way is not often the right way. And when you take the easy way, when you go against what you believe is right, you isolate yourself from your spirit. The challenge boils down to this: With whom do you want to live happily ever after—your associates or yourself ?

It's sometimes hard to know when to take an issue to the mat or let it go. You can't turn every issue into a world war battle. Then again, you can't let them all pass by. My best advice is to listen to your heart. Deep down, you'll always know the right thing to do.

I once found myself staring down a naked emperor while working in corporate America. A new product had just been through the test-marketing phase and was in the process of getting a recommendation for national expansion. I was assigned to write the recommendation.

As my recommendation rose through the many layers of management, I was asked to do additional analysis of the test market results. Something began bugging me. I had been cast in the role of advocate for the product, but I was finding disturbing "blips" in the data.

The recommendation was on the president's desk awaiting approval. About this time, I discovered the brand's volume forecast had been far too generous—in fact, it had been overstated by a factor of two. My problem was that the source of my less-optimistic projections was data derived from grocery-store scanners. At the time, scanners were a brand new, essentially untested system for measuring sales. So no one trusted the new scanner data.

This put me in a corner. The company had dropped $30 million building a plant to make the product and was getting ready to spend $50 million more. More than seventy-five people had been hired to man the new factory. My name was on the expansion recommendation. And there I was, thinking it was the wrong way to go.

If I kept my mouth shut, the brand would be launched across America. In all likelihood, I'd be promoted to another brand before the first year's sales results were in, and I'd be out of there. The problem was compounded by the unproven nature of the source of the data. To add to my angst, Pizza Hut made me a very lucrative offer to lead its new-product efforts.

I tried talking with a number of managers about my concerns. I showed them my data. They reacted with disbelief. There, there, I was told—I was still young, I couldn't see the big picture; I was worrying over nothing.

Their attitude was disturbing and disillusioning. I'd come to believe the company was successful because it was in the habit of doing the right thing even when the right thing was unpopular. After all, the company's vaunted commitment to product safety, quality, and fairness was trumpeted in all its recruiting efforts.

After two weeks of this, I decided that if the company wasn't going to do the right thing in this case, it wasn't the right company for me. I quit. I told my boss I was going to work at Pizza Hut because I didn't like the way the company had received my new findings. Ten minutes later, I was summoned to the office of our division's vice president of marketing—my boss's boss's boss. He invited me to take a seat and told me he'd just heard I was thinking about making pizza for a living. "I'm going to try to talk you out of leaving," he said. "But if I'm unsuccessful, I'm going to lock you in that chair until you tell me about this new data you've found."

Here, at last, was someone interested in what I'd found. I nearly ran back to the my desk to get the data. I passionately explained why the brand I had so ardently endorsed in that same office a few weeks earlier should be eighty-sixed. The big boss listened closely. He wondered if there were any way to validate my new conclusion with more familiar data sources.

I said maybe, but it would require a mountain of work. He asked me if I was interested in doing a mountain of work. I accepted. And in that moment, my pizza career came to a screeching halt. My recommendation was pulled immediately from the president's desk. Working with the best minds in the management-systems division, we did the necessary computations using classical data. Ten practically sleepless days later, the conclusion was the same. By a vote of eight to one, the brand's expansion plan was rejected.

The big boss had restored my faith in the people and culture of the organization. Of course, it was disappointing to know that, in order to prove my conviction, I'd had to be willing to leave the company. But in the end, I had the satisfaction of knowing I'd done the right thing.

The experience had a profound impact on me. I listen closely to minority voices of discontent. I seek out the perspectives of those who go against the pack. I've learned that when you speak out against conventional wisdom and you convince the crowd to move in another direction, you're rewarded with a feeling of immense empowerment.

Think back on your life journey. When and where did you cut against the grain? Maybe it involved a multimillion-dollar business decision. Maybe it was a matter of standing up against a gang of bullies. Either way, what you learn from those experiences is that, once you've survived a few big deals, the little ones are a cinch.

*   *   *

Jim Simmons learned a long time ago not to listen too closely to conventional wisdom. Jim is a travel/adventure writer who lives in San Diego. His story is the best I know of for illustrating why it's not a good idea to pay a whole lot of attention to experts. It's about how he almost went bald and almost died of a brain tumor, but didn't because he took matters into his own hands.

Twenty-four years ago, when Jim was teaching English literature at Boston University, he was diagnosed with a condition that Boston's leading dermatologist told him he could do nothing about—that being "normal male hair loss."

Jim was familiar with this condition, inasmuch as his younger brother, father, and grandfather were all cueballs. All Jim knew was, he didn't want to be a cueball, too. He decided to take an alternative approach. He went to health-food stores, where he learned B-complex vitamins were the key to hair health. So he started taking megadoses of B three times a day. Not only did he stop losing hair, he developed hair on his chest where he never had it before. He had to get haircuts every three weeks instead of every four. And he had to start shaving twice a day.

A few years passed. At the age of fifty-two, Jim developed symptoms of rapidly advancing Alzheimer's disease—loss of short-term memory, general befuddlement, an unsteady gait. At the time, he was living in Cincinnati. Three doctors there told him he had a benign condition of neuropathy, a catch-all term for a disorder of the nervous system. They suggested he buy a cane.

In September, Jim got a second opinion from a neurologist in San Diego. An MRI brain scan revealed a rare type of benign tumor pressing against his brain stem, causing a build-up of intercranial fluid in his brain, a condition known as hydrocephalus. Four days later, Jim underwent surgery to drain the fluid. His doctor later told him that, without the operation, the hydrocephalus would have killed him in another two weeks. But there was still the matter of the tumor.

At that point, Jim took control of his treatment. He spent six weeks at the medical library at the University of California, reading every article he could find about pineocytomas, the technical name for tumors like the one he had. He sent copies of his MRIs to every medical center in America that specialized in the treatment of brain tumors. Then he called the neurosurgeons after they'd had a chance to look at his MRIs. A dozen doctors told him his case was hopeless. Then others recommended a surgical procedure that had a 15 percent risk of blindness, paralysis, or death.

Around that time, Jim heard about something called the gamma knife. "It was a new way to treat brain tumors. A buddy who heads up the *NBC Evening News* bureau in San Francisco sent me a release about it after a gamma knife went on-line at a medical center up there. I immediately took the release to my neurosurgeon, who dismissed it as a gimmick."

Jim didn't. He studied up. He learned that the gamma knife wasn't a knife at all, but a machine with a helmet at one end that looks like an old-fashioned hair dryer; so that when one climbs into it, it zaps the targeted tissue with 201 beams of cobalt-60 photon radiation. There were no bone saws, no opening of the skull, no poking around in soft, gray tissues.

Jim liked that. He called the head brain man at the University of Pittsburgh Medical Center because it had the oldest gamma-knife unit in the country and because it was one of only two hospitals in America with experience handling brain-stem tumors like his.

One October day, Jim climbed into the gamma knife as an out-patient. The next day, he flew back to San Diego alone. Five days later, he was doing the jitterbug, one of the chief passions of his life. Six months later, his tumor had shrunk by 30 percent. The long-term prognosis called for it to disappear eventually.

The way Jim saw it, you can't expect doctors to know everything. Doctors are too busy with their practices to keep up with every new technology that comes along. "So in many cases, it's up to the patient to find out what the alternatives are," Jim said. "A lot of times, you have to find your own way."

Think about it. When have you gone along with the crowd because it was the easy thing to do? When have you stood up and spoken your mind when it was the right thing to do? What did you risk when you did? What were the risks if you hadn't?

If the people around you aren't interested in what you have to say when you know what you have to say is the truth, is it time to go somewhere else?

Build Courage by Plugging Energy Leaks

My grandmother used to say if you can't say anything nice, don't say anything at all. When everyone around you is badmouthing someone who's not there, have the courage to stand in their stead and put in a good word on their behalf. A good word can stop a freight train of ill will. You'll be surprised how many people, by your example, will stand in your stead when you need it most.

HANNAH BUCHANAN

You'll never reach your destination if you're running on empty. That's why it's important to control energy leakage.

I believe we each have a finite amount of energy to carry us through our life journeys—especially in terms of the emotional energy it takes to overcome hardships and endure setbacks. When someone burns out, it's because in large part he or she has depleted his or her emotional energy reserves. When we lose hope or we lose sight of our sense of mission, our energy can quickly evaporate. And when energy evaporates, so does courage.

Energy and courage are an appealing couple. They nurture, reinforce, and bolster each other. If you're filled with one, you're more likely to be filled with the other.

In order to maintain courage, you have to guard your energy zealously. You have to be energy-efficient. One's ability to overcome hurdles and hardships depends to a great extent on one's energy levels, perhaps not to the degree that perseverance hinges on courage and inner strength, but nearly so.

Some people are energy leeches. Beware of those who preface every comment with "Yes, but . . ." They can drain you. Avoid them. If you don't avoid them, push them to focus on the positive. Above all, tolerate no whining.

Negativism can suck energy from you. When you focus on the half empty glass, you put your energy at risk. Even small doses of negativity can erode courage.

You build energy—and stimulate courage—when you focus on the positive. Energy flows from solutions, not problems. You can almost feel the energy leaking from your pores when you contemplate the magnitude of your problems. Instead, aim your energy at discovering solutions.

Beware, too, of those whose modus operandus is to stab you in the back with a roll of the eyes or a shrug of the shoulders. These people are too afraid of conflict to voice their disapproval, so they seek to sap your energy with body language and inflections.

Think of the people, tasks and environments that, for you, are energy builders or energy drains. It's easy to tell the difference. For instance, when you pick up the phone and hear the voice of this person or that person, do you perk up? Or do you wish you'd let your answering machine take the call?

Sometimes, we steal energy from ourselves. Excessive worrying causes us to lose energy. We also lose energy when we lose our tempers. Losing your temper is more like an energy hemorrhage. On the other hand, sometimes it's worse if you don't lose your temper. Either way, anger is one of the worst kinds of energy leeches.

David Wecker has a friend named Bill who has been a writer with an advertising group for seven years. When Bill started, he was a brilliant copywriter. He won a string of prestigious awards, and his work was regularly held up to the rest of the group as the kind of writing they all should aspire to produce for their clients.

One day, Bill's supervisor made a remark about a woman Bill was seeing—and, in fact was quite serious about it at the time, although the relationship has since ended. It was a stupid, uncouth remark, and the supervisor probably would have kept it to himself had he been aware Bill was dating the woman. But the remark infuriated Bill. Instead of approaching his supervisor and possibly resolving the situation, he kept it inside. Over the next few weeks, his anger grew into an intense, unreasoning dislike for the supervisor, to the point that he became obsessed with it. As if to spite his supervisor, Bill let his work slide to a level where it was just barely acceptable.

It's been a long time since Bill's work has been held up as an example of good advertising copy. Other factors have contributed to the situation, but David tells me that the last time he heard from Bill, he was still wearing his anger like a weight around his neck. He'd long since found other things to be angry about. But he had gotten into the habit of nurturing anger. And it had fairly well fogged over the lens through which he viewed the world.

Another way to inflict energy leakages on ourselves is to say "Yes" too much of the time. Usually, when we're saying "Yes" too often, it's to propositions along the lines of:

"I know you're busy, but could you fit just one more teensy-weensy folder in your caseload?"

Or "Say, you look like you've just about recovered from that case of pneumonia. How about if you take my Friday night shift? It would mean overtime for you."

Or "I'm having trouble making progress on this account. How about if you handle it for me? I'd owe you one."

The best antidote for too many "Yesses" is to learn to say "No" once in a while. It's human nature to want to be liked—which is why when people ask for our time and energy, we too often end up saying yes even when we can't realistically deliver without undergoing a whole lot of stress.

Saying yes to helping someone else is a worthy aim. Saying yes to a request or a demand that threatens to push you past the limits of your energy is the wrong thing to do.

Saying no can sometimes be the only way to say yes to your dream. But the social pressures against saying no can be as intense as the pressures to conform to established points of view. Most of the time, these social pressures are presented in the form of a question that revolves around one of the following themes:

"Could you drop me off in Boston on your way to Cleveland? It's only eleven hours out of your way."

Or, "You love me, don't you? Come on over here!"

Or, "You want some of this or not? What are you? Chicken?"

Or, "What are you waiting for? Don't you know everybody does it?"

When you say no to someone who has asked you either to go unreasonably out of your way or to join him or her in something that doesn't feel right to you, you're simply reinforcing the value of your previous personal commitments. If you take responsibility for requests beyond your abilities, you'll shortchange something somewhere along the line. If you respond to a request merely on the basis of social pressure, you're shortchanging yourself. In either case, saying no doesn't mean you're a slackard; it means you have a sense of mission, values, and personal responsibility.

Let's practice. Go ahead. Say it now. On your mark, get set . . .

"NO!"

Not bad. Now, let's try some variations. "I'm sorry, but I can't right now." Or "I'm sorry, but I can't devote the energy it would take to fulfill your request." Or "I could, but I'll be much better off if I don't—so I won't."

Sometimes, you don't have to actually say no. Sometimes you can get the point across with "I'd rather eat a Junebug."

Now consider ways to generate energy around you. One way is to show respect for others' efforts. Opportunities to do this present themselves all the time.

I once invited an entire development team to put their signatures on the inside flap of a new product we designed together. Another time, working with a flavor company on a beverage product, I had the flavorists inscribe their names on the bottles. In each case, the act of putting their signatures on the product generated energy for the whole team—energy that gave each team member more enthusiasm and courage to deal with subsequent issues in their respective endeavors.

If you care about the people you work with, it shows. They'll feel it and respond in kind. Look for reasons to bestow praise. Let the people you work with know they're appreciated. Pretty soon, they'll be falling on grenades for you.

But don't lavish laurels for that reason. Do it because it's the right thing to do.

You generate energy when you do good for people who are in real need. Giving of yourself to others is one of the most effective ways of generating personal energy. And it fills you with a feeling of satisfaction for having shined a light.

My grandmother is a master at donating her time and support. She has made a habit of praying for and otherwise looking after several families in the rural Maine countryside where she lives.

When she hears of a single mother who's having trouble keeping her children in warm clothing, for instance, she takes her to a church sale where she can find clean secondhand coats, hats, and mittens. "The mothers are so thankful," she says. "But it's as much a blessing to me to see their children in warm clothing."

Look back. What have you done to help someone in need? What unexpected kindnesses could you perform in your community, for your friends, your family or a stranger who, with a little help, could get back on his feet?

Go ahead. Reach out. Give someone a little boost. You'll get more than you give.

Grow or Die

An act of courage can change one's life and that, perhaps, is what we fear most.

WALT HARRELL

O n each of your life's journeys, you're either nurturing courage and experiencing new wonders or you're merely letting your life elapse. It's a matter of grow or die.

As long as you're growing, you're free. If you choose to subordinate your life to something you don't believe in because it's less of a strain or it's lucrative or it's what others expect of you, you'll lose yourself. Slowly but surely, a piece of you will fade away each day.

When you grow, you gain strength. Imagine an acorn falling to the forest floor. It sprouts, develops into a seedling and begins pushing toward the sky, growing taller and stronger, sprouting new shoots and leaves with each passing year. The taller the tree grows, the more resistant it becomes to disease, the better it's able to handle droughts. Its limbs continue to reach upward until the day it dies. If you live a growth-oriented life, then you, too, will find the strength necessary to overcome the inevitable adversities that go along with having a pulse.

The natural order of a tree is continuous growth. It cannot suspend its own growth. Each season, it must add another ring to its girth, sprout new buds, push its roots deeper into the earth.

People are like trees in that we have the ability to vegetate. People are unlike trees in that we can also cogitate. Cogitating has its good points and its bad points. It gives us the ability to control our orientation; that is, the ways and directions in which we grow. But it also gives us the capacity, however unconsciously, to imagine that we can suspend our growth, plant ourselves right where we are, and maintain a seated position from here on in, preferably on a comfy couch. This often occurs during some stage of adulthood.

When we're children, we embrace growth. We eagerly learn to walk, to talk, and to let our needs be known. When we turn six, we can't wait to be eight. When we're eight, we can't wait to be ten. But as we progress from wanting to be older to wishing we were young again, we think we can stop changing, stop growing, and stay right where we are. But when we voluntarily stop growing, we pay a terrible price. We trade growth for death.

When we give up on growing, we become slaves to conformity and mediocrity. We exchange an aggressive love of life for a life lived on the defensive. When we consign ourselves to slavery, we apply courage to protecting what we are and what we have instead of using it as a tool for growth. We spend our courage fighting fears instead of stimulating growth. But as long as you're growing, you're free.

Freedom is an abstract concept. Like the wind, you can't see it or touch it. But you know it's there because you can feel it. You can feel its presence, and you can feel its absence. Freedom makes it possible to go one-on-one with the world. Freedom makes it possible for one person to make a difference—just as believing it's possible makes it possible. When you're free, you elevate yourself from being a faceless member in a faceless society to an individual with a dream.

Once upon a time in America, the importance of freedom was drummed into our heads. The willingness to die for freedom was programmed into the hearts of America's school children. Little boys wanted to grow up to be John Wayne, with the inner strength to pay the ultimate price on some desolate foreign shore so their families would never have to worry about being free.

Somewhere along the line, all that changed. Once we began taking freedom for granted, it became less precious. Instead of remaining eternally vigilant, America became a nation of eternal compromisers. In the process, we traded freedom for convenience. We sold ourselves into slavery, in all its many forms—slavery to our fears; slavery to established thinking, whether it's right or wrong; slavery to always take the path of least resistance; slavery to preconceived notions of who we are and what we are. For too many of us, it has become acceptable to give up with out a fight.

Today, America is in an era of voluntary slavery. We've learned to curl up and blame our problems on external circumstances. The tragedy is that no one forced us at bayonet point to give up our dreams and ideals; the tragedy is that we've surrendered them. Individually and collectively, we've relinquished the power to determine how we think to whatever winds happen to be blowing through the culture at the moment. As our values become blurred, our lives spin out of control.

It takes courage to break the bonds, step forward and take a chance on a dream you've been trying to ignore. But the consequences of remaining in a state of voluntary slavery and doing nothing should terrify you. It's a short step from taking your freedom for granted to taking your life for granted. It's another short step to looking back on your life and realizing you let it slip through your fingers.

One way to find life is to come close to losing it. There's nothing like a near-death experience to rearrange your priorities. Standing at the edge of death has a humbling effect—and a way of clarifying and reminding you of what life should be all about.

I've never been there myself. I'd barely even thought about death and dying until I became involved in a pair of projects— first, creating ideas for the Batesville Casket Company, the world's largest manufacturer of caskets, and a few months after that, creating ideas for one of its sister companies, Forethought Life Insurance, which is in the business of helping people make funeral arrangements before they die.

Before these projects came along, I thought preplanned funerals were for brain-dead people who had nothing whatsoever going on in their lives. In my former way of thinking, one casket was the same as another; the object was to spend as little time and money as possible picking one out—and then only when it absolutely couldn't be put off any longer.

I wasn't alone. In fact, I had trouble finding people willing to work with me on either project, largely because they were reluctant to deal, even tangentially, with the subjects of funerals, caskets and death.

But as my team listened to the executives from Batesville and Forethought discuss death and dying, and about funerals as an emotional healing tool for the living, the subject of death became less remote to us. As it became less remote, it became less distasteful.

We came to see how the notion of planning a funeral ahead of time wasn't at all inconsistent with a three-dimensional love of life. We realized, in fact, it implied a profound inner peace. The more we reflected on death, the more energized we became about our lives. We talked about what we'd want for our funerals and about the sorts of symbols that would be emblematic of our own lives. And as we discussed our deaths, we became energized about living life to the fullest.

Joyce Meier had a firsthand understanding of the paradox. She says many of her friends can't comprehend why she'd want to be a volunteer at Hospice of Cincinnati. "You learn more about the living by working with the dying than you could ever learn by working with the living," she says. In the dying, Joyce sees healings.

"A tremendous amount of healing occurs when a person is terminally ill. Healing means becoming whole. You can lose control or function in your body but still be whole spiritually, mentally, emotionally."

Think about your funeral. If you were to die tomorrow, how would you want your obituary to read? How would you be remembered? How is the way you would be remembered different from how you'd like to be remembered? What moments have defined your life? What are you proudest of? What are you the least proud of? What kind of person have you been?

Be honest. Are you pleased with how you turned out? Are you satisfied you made the most of the time you've had? Or do you find yourself wanting?

Take heart. Your life isn't over yet. There's time to make changes.

Try this. Imagine you're in a universe parallel to Charles Dickens's A *Christmas Carol* and you're traveling through time with the ghosts of your past. Drift back to one or two of your defining moments from childhood. What voices and images come to mind? Why? What expectations did your parents, grandparents, teachers, coaches, spouses, kids, bosses, or friends have for you? How were you stereotyped? How did these stereotypes help you grow? How did they impede your growth? How did you allow yourself to be shaped by them? Why?

Search through your memory banks for one or two defining moments from your teenage years and ask yourself the same questions. Think of a defining moment as any experience, whether it occurred in a literal moment or over an extended period, that had an impact on the person you have become.

Now fast forward to a decade or even a year ago and repeat the process.

Compare your defining moments. When in your life were you most courageous? At what times in your life were you more willing to take on new challenges? Why? What factors diminished or strengthened your courage? Can you find a specific point in time when you make the decision to fall into step because it was easier than standing alone?

Contrast the ghosts of your past with the person you are—especially in terms of your relative levels of confidence and ability. Are you advancing on life, or are you retreating from it?

Or are you exactly the same person you were a year or two or three ago? Are you doing basically the same things in the same ways, facing the same set of fears with no sign of change on the horizon?

If this is the case, it's time to grow. It's time to take action.

When I was in the seventh grade, I broke my hip in a football game. I spent most of the next two years in a full-body cast at Boston Children's Hospital, in a reclining position in the family room at home, or on crutches at school.

The accident set me apart. It forced me to go through the pubescent process of self-discovery pretty much on my own. While other kids were traveling in clusters, going to dances and basketball games and generally finding out about life in groups, I was off by myself trying to figure out who I was. I learned to rely on myself and not to expect a whole lot from others. Because I was isolated by my circumstances, peer pressure wasn't a factor.

As is often the case, what appeared at first to be a setback turned out to be a blessing. I had time to think—and the opportunity to let whatever was inside me emerge without being pushed or pulled by external influences.

I began to study magic because it was something I could do in a prone position. By the time I could get around on crutches, I was a fairly decent vaudeville-type performer and a dedicated entrepreneur. As a ninth grader, I scraped together $50 I earned shoveling snow and launched my first business, an enterprise that revolved around the manufacture and sale of learn-to-juggle kits. It was the beginning of what, today, has grown into a multimillion-dollar company.

I had friends, but I was by no means part of the in crowd. I was, in the parlance of the day, "out there." I was the kid who juggled flaming torches at halftime of the football game; the kid who published the underground newspaper that made fun of everything that happened in the hallowed halls of Nashua High; the kid who levitated a girl high atop the tallest building in Nashua, New Hampshire, and talked the local newspaper into running a photo with the caption, "The Highest Levitation in New England." I was an independent spirit in a world of teenage conformity. I followed my own interests and actively looked for opportunities to stick out my neck for the sake of being myself.

Isn't it a shame? We think of the teenage years as a time of independence, self-discovery, and rebellion. The truth is, most teenagers trade one kind of conformity for another—the conformity imposed on them as a natural consequence of living under their parents' roofs for the conformity that accompanies peer pressure. Few teenagers leave much room in their lives for true self-expression and discovery. For that matter, neither do many grown-ups.

I was fortunate. Because of a football injury, I was channeled into being independent. I was able to develop independently of any influence I didn't invite into my life. Sometimes, I wonder how I would have turned out if I hadn't had that advantage.

I'm amazed at how completely time heals pain. Even the most mortifying failures of my early years—the magic tricks that fell apart onstage, the business concepts that went belly-up, the girls who dumped me, a disastrous French horn solo my senior year and that regrettable beer party in my parents' basement when they weren't home—are now golden memories. Events that once threatened to bring about the end of my life turned out to be growth steps in the journey toward a life worth living.

Twenty years from now, today's failures will be shimmering memories. You may recall the pain they caused, and you might cringe at the memory. But you'll also see how they helped you move forward.

If you're having trouble drumming up the courage to be free, step back from the here and now. Look beyond your immediate circumstances at the big picture. Take some time to watch the planets spin.

It's all right to feel badly about today's failures. If we don't grieve over our failures, we're destined to repeat them. Instead, learn from them. But once you've learned, let them go. And realize that, over the long haul, they'll look a whole lot different to you than they do now.

Bob Egner—who lives in Guilford, Indiana, and who is the father of a twenty-four-year-old mentally retarded daughter—learned a rhyme from his mother that he calls on for perspective in dark moments:

> *From the day you are born*
> *'til you ride in a hearse,*
> *things are never so bad*
> *that they couldn't get worse.*

You're the Only One Responsible for You

When you point a finger at someone, three fingers point back at you.

STEVE FRIEDBERG

In our culture, whining is fashionable. Like hypochondriacs, we compare notes on our suffering. "You think you've got it bad," we say. "Wait until you get a load of this . . ."

The eleven o'clock news is fraught with stories about so-called injustices and so-called victims blaming their problems on evil forces at work in their lives. The offices of psychologists and psychiatrists are filled with people seeking to resolve inequities imposed on them by their environments. We've become a world of finger-pointers and blame-fixers.

When two or more people gather, you'll often hear whining. The next time you're out somewhere having lunch, eavesdrop on the conversations around you. From kindergarten cafeterias to factory lunchrooms, from fast-food restaurants to country-club dining rooms, whining knows no social class. Listen to how negative it is. Notice how it leads nowhere. All it seems to do is perpetuate itself.

Sooner or later, when two or more people are engaged in mutual whining, one of them makes this observation: "It's not *fair*."

This is as close as most whining ever gets to the truth, but it doesn't carry the concept far enough. The hairless naked truth is this: Life isn't fair. Who told them it would be? When they emerged into the world, no government official was waiting to hand them a written guarantee that life would be fair. No regulatory agency ever decreed that, inasmuch as they never asked to be born, there's some sort of cosmic scale that balances out all the factors in life, so that for every bad thing that happens to them, something good happens, too.

Look at it another way. Now is the best time in the history of the planet to be alive. Never has there been more opportunity for the ordinary man or woman to have an impact on the world. To succeed in business fifty years ago, you had to have a ton of money to build a factory. If you had been a woman or a minority member half a century ago, it would have been all but impossible even to pursue interests beyond the boundaries society imposed on you.

It's a brave new world. And it's never been smaller. The personal computer and the Internet have empowered the individual. Where it was once a capital-intensive world of steel mills and assembly lines, it has become a world of ideas and personal vision. To succeed in today's world, you don't need millions of dollars. All you need is imagination and courage.

This is not to say that changing one's attitude is a simple matter. It's much easier to let the gravitational pull of mediocrity hold you back. As a people, we've come to expect we're owed something. This feeling has become more prevalent as we've become more economically successful, particularly in the United States. We have developed the mistaken notion that, if the nation is experiencing an economic upswing, we deserve our cut—when, in fact, we're owed nothing that we haven't earned.

This kind of thinking adds up to a collective unwillingness to take responsibility. For most of us, taking responsibility is an unnatural act. When we fall short, instead of owning up and saying, "I was wrong," we point fingers anywhere but at ourselves. In so doing, we relinquish control of our lives. If you aren't willing to take responsibility when you lose, you deserve no credit when you win.

The whole time we're avoiding responsibility, we're consumed with avoiding failure at all costs. We take the easy way out. We avoid failure by avoiding challenges. When opportunity knocks, we call the locksmith and have him install another deadbolt. We steer clear of opportunities that present any risk.

And on those increasingly rare occasions when we do act on an opportunity, we give it less than our best effort. Our lack of courage requires instant success. And if at first we don't succeed, we quit. The concept of failing a few times, persevering, and then finally succeeding has become quaint, old-fashioned, and passé.

If you have a dream, there's no justification for exerting anything less than your total effort to make it happen. Likewise, there's no justification for resorting to excuses when you fall on your face—whether it's racism, sexism, or educational snobbery. As a white male, I'll probably never experience the first two. But I've bumped up against the third.

When I started at P&G in marketing, I was one of very few new hires in the division who'd never taken a college-accredited business course—or any business course at all, for that matter. I was a chemical engineer from a small public school, and the only business training I had, had come through having operated my own businesses since the age of twelve, whether that meant performing as a juggler and magician at county fairs throughout New England or selling advertising space on vinyl telephone-book covers as a student at the University of Maine.

In short, I did not have the sort of background that typically

raises the eyebrows of P&G recruiters. P&G's advertising department tends to seek out MBAs from such institutions of higher
learning as Harvard, Northwestern, and Darden. It is a company
that prides itself on hiring the best and the brightest: kids in
tailor-made suits who set records with their SAT scores, trained ex-
tensively in the job interviewing process, and graduated Magna-
Cum-You'd-Better-Hire-Me-Before-the-Competition-Does.

When I arrived for my interview dressed in a clean but frumpy
suit I'd purchased off the sale rack, I was unburdened with any
such credentials. My pockets were stuffed with my Magic Bunny
trick, an illusion by which tiny sponge rabbits seemed to multiply
as if by magic. Tucked under my arm was a scrapbook of newspaper clips and photographs from my magic show and my small-
business exploits on campus.

I was feeling smart and jaunty as I signed in at the reception
desk at Sixth and Sycamore in downtown Cincinnati and was
ushered into an eighth floor conference room to await my interviews. Two other prospective P&G employees, one of each gender,
both far better dressed than I, were also awaiting interviews. I introduced myself. "Hi, how ya doin'?" I said. Their responses were,
well, distant. "So," I said to the woman, "where did you go to
school?" She replied that she was a graduate of Northwestern
Business School. I turned to the male prospect and asked him the
same question. He told me he went to school in Boston.

"Boston?" I asked. "Where in Boston?" To which, he replied
curtly, "Cambridge."

"Oh," I said innocently, failing to make the connection between Cambridge and Harvard. "Where in Cambridge exactly?"
The B School, he said in a tone of bored exasperation. At that
point, he asked me where I had received my education.

"Orono," I said proudly. I could see I was drawing a blank.
Orono?

"You know—Orono, *Maine*," I said, my confidence experiencing a sudden puncture. "*Orono*, the home of the *University* of Maine. That's where I got my degree—a *bachelor's* in chemical engin*eering*."

As long as I live, I'll never forget his expression of complete disdain, punctuated with a contemptuous roll of his eyes. It hit me like a kick in the gut. I rethought my strategy. It occurred to me that I had a fat nerve being there in the first place. What made me think I had a chance with the company that invented modern brand marketing? Who did I think I was? For crying out loud!

I swallowed hard. I sat there in my pool of flop sweat and ruled out options. Clearly, it was too late to run out and buy a more expensive suit. It was too late to change who I was or where I'd been. My only option was to be me and do what I do best. So I did. When it was time for my interview, I performed a few sleight-of-hand illusions and went beyond the bounds of professionally acceptable levels of energy, enthusiasm, and passion in my zeal to sell Doug Hall to Procter & Gamble.

I got the job. Later that day on the way home, I bumped into the Harvard grad at the Greater Cincinnati International Airport. Assuming that he, too, had received a job offer, I asked how soon he'd be moving to Cincinnati. He explained in his most professional manner that P&G would be getting back to him. He hadn't gotten a job. Honestly, I was amazed. The guy was a pro. I was sure of it. But maybe he was too much of a pro. Maybe somewhere along the line, he forgot how to be himself.

All I'd been was me—a hyperkinetic bundle of raw energy, commitment, and passion. It was my only option. It was also the best option. In lieu of academic credentials, I worked hard—and I used what I had. And that sufficed. It's like Ben Franklin said— God helps those who help themselves.

It's up to you. If you want to be somebody, you're the only

body who can make it happen. To get there, which requires over-coming your fears and taking that first step, you have to find within yourself the capacity to give yourself a serious butt-kicking now and then. After all, you've gone to great lengths to nurture and cultivate your fears; they aren't likely to wither away on their own. And trust me on this—you'll end up feeling better for hav-ing done it.

But please—don't confuse fear with laziness, whining, or inac-tion. It doesn't matter how bad you have it. We all have hard-ships. As long as you have a pulse, bad things are bound to happen to you. In fact, a life consisting exclusively of good things would be boring. Adam and Eve lived in utopian surroundings, and they couldn't handle it. The bad things that happen to us make it pos-sible for us to appreciate the good things. They keep life from be-ing a flat, horizontal line. Without pain, we wouldn't know how to hope or feel elation or pleasure.

Learn to take responsibility for yourself NOW!

How?

- Start living in the present tense. Stop dwelling on what happened yesterday. Don't think about what could or should or would have been. What's the point? It's wasted energy. Concentrate on what you can do today and what tomorrow can offer.
- Stop measuring yourself by the standards of others. No matter what you achieve or how often you've failed, you'll never be the best or the worst. Your life journey is a relative experience. Each of your competitors has strengths and weaknesses in varying proportions to your strengths and weaknesses. Start with what you have and grow from there.
- Take action—any action. If you do nothing, nothing will

change. If you do the same old stuff, you'll end up with the same old results. The only way to change your situation is to take responsibility and try something different. And if you're going nowhere, you'll continue to go nowhere until you do something.

As we travel through life, we collect positive and negative baggage. If you aren't careful, you can get so bogged down with negative baggage that it wears away your confidence. It doesn't have to be that way. It's up to you to take personal responsibility to decide what to hold on to—and what isn't worth carrying any further.

Life's Many Journeys

*When I get scared, I look back and say "I was
able to do such and such before." If that
doesn't work, I imagine it's my last day on
earth. That usually gets me moving!*

MERRY GENG, AGE 37

We travel many journeys in our lives. We live concurrent
lives as parents, workers, spouses, children, and members
of the community. Each journey is different. Our
progress, maturity, courage and confidence vary from one to another. We may be pillars of courage and confidence in terms of
how we bring up our children, and whimpering pools of trepida-
tion when it comes to our jobs. Or vice versa. Accepting and understanding this can help us grow.

It's different for children. As children, we set out on a single
journey—to reach out with both hands and discover as much as
we can about the world. As children, we think of ourselves as
equally adept at art, acting, basketball, running fast, and climbing
trees.

This inborn willingness to set out on a diverse range of different journeys all at the same time fades as we grow older. We become positively or negatively reinforced through our experiences
and by our peers so that, by the time we arrive at adulthood, our
vision is funneled down to a pinpoint. Somewhere along the line,

we decide to pursue only those journeys and endeavors where we know we'll succeed.

We focus on a few areas at the expense of all others. Where once we saw a world filled with possibilities, we look at life through the wrong end of the binoculars. We limit our possibilities because limiting possibilities makes us feel safer. Too often, we wonder why we feel our lives bottoming out, forgetting we made the decisions that put us in shallow water.

I've caught myself on several occasions concentrating on one journey at the complete expense of all others. When I left the corporate world and launched my company, I was a virtual hermit, living in my basement for months on end, for eighteen hours a day and more. I had no time for anything that wasn't linked directly to building the business. All that focus on my "career" journey made the company successful—but at the cost of neglecting my wife and children. I lost moments with my family I can never recover.

The pendulum swung. My priorities shifted and I spent less time on the business, to the point of shirking responsibilities. I became obsessed with family. Like a lot of people, I have to explore the extremes before I can begin to find a comfortable middle ground.

Once when Debbie and I were sifting through our memories, she got to talking about the ways I'd changed over the years. She reminded me of how, when we met as high school students, I had all kinds of hobbies and interests. She ticked them off on her fingers: I was in the marching band, played on all kinds of sports teams, had my own traveling magic and juggling act, kept up a busy schedule with the Boy Scouts.

"But look at you now," she said, not as disapprovingly, perhaps, as I'm making it sound—but she allowed as to how I was altogether hobby-less. My life had become my work and my family. She was right. At that moment, I didn't have nearly the range of interests I once had. I'd narrowed my focus to only two journeys. My net worth in dollars and cents was growing, but my wealth in life experiences and enjoyment was declining. I resolved to do something. To explore hobbies. To spend more time on areas apart from work, digging into subjects that might stretch my mind.

This was no simple matter. When your thinking has been pointed in one and only one direction over a period of months and years, it's difficult to get off that track—even if only to touch whatever might be to the immediate right or immediate left of you.

Often when people retire, they make the same discovery. They've worked hard for years, only to come face to face with too many choices, too much time. Many seniors, particularly career professionals whose identities are too tied up in their job descriptions, go through painful periods of depression and uncertainty when the retire. They find themselves with more time than goals. All of a sudden, they no longer have a reason to get out of bed in the morning.

My grandmother never had this problem. After forty-one years as a public school teacher and forty years as a church organist, she retired at the age of sixty. Instead of slowing down, she picked up the pace. She bought a shell of a farmhouse, rebuilt it with my grandfather, and put in a big garden filled with vegetables and flowers. She also took classes in cake decorating, decoupage, knitting, reverse painting, and rug braiding, twisting together more than 100 rugs to date. At eighty-eight, her eyesight isn't what it used to be. But she doesn't let that prevent her from traveling a wide range of life journeys.

Around the time I was coming to realize how I'd narrowed down my own life journeys, I met a retired couple who stood in sharp contrast to my grandmother. I was in Florida playing golf with a friend. By chance, he and I ended up in a foursome with this newly retired couple. He had recently retired from an executive position. Early on, it became apparent he was not a happy man. I tried to draw him out with a few observations about what a pretty day it was and a few comments about my lousy golf game. But he was bound and determined to sulk.

On the tenth hole, as I was walking up the fairway with his wife, she told me he'd been retired only three months and that he was driving her and everyone else they knew out of their minds. He had nothing to do with all the time he suddenly had on his hands, and he was miserable because of it.

I looked at him and saw myself thirty years from that point wearing the same sour expression on my face. And I knew that if nothing in my life changed, I'd end up that way. It was precisely the syndrome I wanted to avoid—and why I embarked on a campaign to find new areas of exploration as intently as I did.

Aboard a jet cruising over the Midwest to visit a client, I pondered the challenge. I wanted to look into areas I could feel passionate about. But what? What interests could I take up that would inspire me to devote the time required to get to know something about them? The niggling thing about starting a new life journey—whether it involves discovering a new interest, aligning yourself with a social movement or initiating a personal improvement plan—is that it requires you to start at the beginning. That means putting yourself at risk, the risk being failure. It takes courage to face up to new beginnings—for many of us, because the experience forces us to admit again that we don't have all the answers.

As I traveled through the clouds, I put together these targets:

- Learn enough about soccer to coach my children's teams.
- Start a collection of red wine, strictly for sipping pur-
  poses.
- Get into photography and set about to capturing some of
  the striking images the world dishes up every day.
- Create a nonprofit foundation, using the services my
  company provides regular clients and applying them to
  charitable causes, with the goal of perhaps in a small way
  making the world a better place.

Each began as a thought that arose from different circumstances, through different conversations with different people at
different times. Each started as a seed of interest that had been
germinating for some time.

I set as an umbrella goal over each of these hobbies to involve
my family as much as possible. It was a natural progression—kids
make good subjects for photos, the whole family loves soccer, and
wine is a natural complement to romantic dinners with my wife.
The idea wasn't to make my hobbies their hobbies, but to provide
open doors through which my family and I could become more
involved in each other's lives.

I've made progress in each of these areas. I've coached my kids'
soccer teams, built a wine cellar and filled it with wonderful wines
and taken hundreds of pictures of the kids and the world around
me. And I've created Planet Eureka!: Ideas for a Better World, a
foundation to help nonprofit organizations develop ideas and
strategies of the same caliber as those we provide our client corporations. The result is that entire new dimensions have been
added to my life, well beyond my work. And my business is no

worse for the wear. In many cases, my peripheral pursuits have enabled me to bring new perspectives to client solutions.

As you sort through your life journeys and assign priorities to them, maintain your balance and leverage your strengths. As Ben Franklin said, "Wealth is not his that has it, but his who enjoys it."

Think about the journeys in your life. What progress are you making in each of them? Where are you succeeding? Where are you marking time? What journeys have you avoided for fear of failure?

Success is seldom an end in itself. It's often hollow. It can leave you asking yourself, "What now? What do I do with this?" Sometimes, you can find a way to translate success into a new life journey, one that fulfills the longing inside you to make a difference, in whatever form it might take. This is what Sam Wyche did with his success.

He embarked on a new life journey one night in 1988, two weeks after leading the Cincinnati Bengals to the Super Bowl. He was a man with a high profile and considerable influence; a famous professional-sports figure with a big home in the suburbs and a sense of obligation to share his good fortune. On this night, he declared his intention to do exactly that.

He traveled to the poor side of town to have dinner at a shelter for the homeless, St. Joseph's House of Hospitality, with a half-dozen men whose lives had fallen apart. He wanted to hear their stories, to encourage them. He had been thinking about men like these for some time now. He wanted to play a small part in helping them turn their lives around. He knew that, if he could do that, he would grow, too.

He saw a way to help Cincinnati's homeless after the Bengals won the American Football Conference Central Division title. It was the beginning of a new life journey.

"Suddenly, there I was, a hot item. Corporations started calling, asking me to speak at sales meetings, seminars, banquets. I've done that kind of thing before—normally, I'd get a nice pat on the back afterwards. Or maybe a pen and pencil set. This year, the price has gone up."

Now, in the afterglow of a division title, the price was $5,000. Companies were paying it, too, just for the chance to rub elbows with a Super Bowl coach. But he didn't see any of that money. Instead, he'd tell the company to send a certain amount to this shelter and a certain amount to that—as long as it had something to do with helping Cincinnati's homeless.

He passed a platter of fried chicken around the table at St. Joe's and listened to the men's stories. Jeff, a journeyman mechanic, lost his job doing six months for DUI. Robert, who had a history of psychological problems, lived on the banks of the Ohio River for two years. Toby's head was crushed in a car crash; when he got out of the hospital a year later, his wife, his savings, and his job were gone.

Sam Wyche talked about the empty buildings downtown and about what it would take to fix them up and make them affordable for people who had no roofs over their heads. He talked about how someone can live on the street and still be an important person. He said he wished he could do more than scratch the surface.

The men who shared their table with him thought he was doing more. They knew he could be spending the evening with his family. They realized he didn't have to give St. Joe's $9,000 so they could have decent bathrooms.

"Here's a guy who's on top of the world—a guy who could turn his back and no one would blame him," Toby said. "And here he is, worried about me."

He didn't win the Super Bowl that year. But he embarked on another journey far removed from his role as an NFL coach, one that had an impact on people's lives more real and more meaningful than any Super Bowl title ever could.

Quality of Life Versus
Ease of Life

It's like getting your teeth drilled at the den-
tist. You're uncomfortable, but you know it
will end. You endure. Sometimes courage is
simply endurance.

ELLEN GUIDERA, AGE 38

A s we achieve middle age, many of us come to the hollow realization that we're leading lives of unfulfilled dreams. We
panic, with good reason. Psychologists call it a midlife crisis.
It's a time when we ask questions about purpose. Generally,
they're the same questions we asked when we were in our twen-
ties—except that, by the time we'd be in our forties, we expected
we'd have the answers and it's killing us that we don't.

You can see it in our collective need to believe in something,
anything. From the advent of psychic hotlines to the New Age
movement to mega-churches with Broadway-worthy musical pro-
ductions, people everywhere are searching for something to believe in that's larger than themselves. They're looking for a way to
make sense of things and a place where they can have purpose. It's
difficult to have that sense of purpose in the absence of courage.
Having real courage is about leading a life uncluttered with regrets, a life where you aren't constantly looking back and saying I
should have, I could have, or I wish I had. Having courage is about

setting a goal, then pursuing it. But not just any goal. When you set a goal, beware of averageness. Avoid averageness as if it had tentacles and exhaled sulphurous flames. Being average is acceptable when it comes to shirt sizes, but it's not a reasonable personal goal. A far better goal, one worth applying to even your smallest endeavors, is to have an impact, make a difference and leave wherever you go a better place.

Maybe you won't be an Albert Sabin and discover a cure for polio. Maybe you won't be a George Washington or a Mahatma Ghandi or a Martin Luther King Jr. and lead a revolution. Maybe not. But you don't have to go down in history to make the world a better place.

As we age, our focus tends to shift from living a quality life to making our lives easy. We set out with high-minded ideals, bump our heads against a few brick walls and gradually come to decide our ideals are naive and foolish. We seek to smooth out rough edges. We buy "new and improved" products based on the premise that they'll make life more convenient.

As time wears on and idealism wears down, we're tempted to take the paths of least resistance. At some point, we decide we've gone as far as we're going to go. We stop taking risks and settle into ruts, dwelling on our pensions, marking time to retirement and escaping the day-to-day world. We give up on ourselves. And we're surprised when everyone else gives up on us, too.

We make fatalistic excuses about the circumstances that have caused us to limit ourselves so severely. Soon, we develop symptoms of a kind of walking rigor mortis. Our joints stiffen, our vertebrae calcify, our limbs atrophy and our vision blurs. Meanwhile, our wills grow softer and softer—to the point that movement becomes increasingly painful. The longer this condition is allowed to exist, the less likely change becomes.

There's a better way.

Think of your life as a football game. Maybe you didn't do so well in the first half. Maybe you dropped the ball every time you got your hands on it. Maybe you were sacked a dozen times and intercepted a dozen more.

The first half is history. Right now, it's a whole new world. Because right now, the second half begins. This is the time to stand up and make a new beginning. Don't save yourself for some future challenge that you imagine will be more important. The moment—the here and now of your life—is assured to you; tomorrow is not.

Ernest Hemingway once was quoted in *The New Yorker* as saying: "It is better to die on your feet than live on your knees." What it all boils down to is balancing Quality of Life against Quick & Convenient. You can opt for an easy life and let yourself be pulled by the forces of conformity—in which case, you'll do nothing. Or you can struggle against the tide and experience the very real anxieties that go along with taking a chance on something you believe in, thereby running the risk of succeeding.

If you're in sync with your values, you'll take the latter course. If you choose causes you're convinced are right, you'll have courage. You'll have an impact, and you'll leave a mark. Most of all, you'll have a life of quality.

To get there, you have to trust your heart as well as your mind. Your mind will sort through the risks; your heart will tell you what's right. When you listen to your heart, you'll find the courage to do the right thing, even when the right thing has negative consequences.

Admittedly, it's easier said than done. We're taught in school that the objective is to get the single correct answer—the right, rational, logical answer. But your heart rules your passions. Your heart is where courage resides.

*   *   *

Cecil Carpenter had the courage to follow his heart. He paid a price because of it. But in his heart, he knew it was the right thing to do. Once he'd made that decision, he had no fear. As for Alex, he went along with Cecil because, basically, he had no choice.

The life went out of Cecil and Alex at the Drawbridge Motor Inn in Fort Mitchell, Kentucky, one day in June. They'd made the trip from Richmond, Indiana, the day before to attend the National Ventriloquists Association's yearly convention. They'd just completed a routine during the open-mike session when the end came.

Cecil was one of the convention crowd's favorites. "Everyone would crowd into the room to see him," said Dorothy Millure, curator of Vent Haven Museum, a nearby shrine to ventriloquism. "He had an unusual act—a spoof of a ventriloquist's act. He would have Alex's mouth moving at the wrong time or he'd mix up Alex's lines with his own or whatever. The schtick was, things would not go well for Cecil. But it was cleverly done, very entertaining. People loved it."

It was hot under the lights. And Cecil wasn't feeling well. He'd been laid up the previous three weeks at St. Vincent Hospital in Indianapolis with heart trouble. He had to sit down a few times during the show, apologizing to the audience for slurring a word here and there. But there would have been no way to keep him off the stage. He'd decided to spend what time he had left doing what he loved, rather than retreating into the haze of convalescence. Cecil insisted on participating in his life. So he finished the routine. When he stepped offstage, his heart gave out. He was fifty-four.

There's no way to know for sure, but it's reasonable to assume Cecil felt pains in his chest before and during the performance.

We do know that the word at the convention was that Cecil had told someone who had told someone who had told someone else that he might not have much time. He could have sat out the performance. He could have settled for sitting in the audience. But he'd made a choice.

The family decided to put Cecil and Alex to rest in the same grave. They were laid out in matching black tuxedos, white ruffled shirts and black bow ties. Five hundred people signed the guest registry at the funeral home. The minister said a few words about Cecil and Alex, about how they had brought many smiles to many people. And when the casket lid was finally closed, it closed over both of them. Cecil would have wanted it that way.

Cecil weighed the consequences. He could give it up, take it easy and probably live a few years longer. Or he could continue to do what he loved doing, going onstage in a black tuxedo, standing in the glare of the footlights and giving strangers something to laugh about. He could continue to wring quality and fulfillment from life. To Cecil, it wasn't much of a choice at all.

What about you? Would you trade five years of fear-filled desperation for a year of freedom? Five years of meaningless tedium for a year of real significance? Five years of doing nothing for a year of doing whatever it is that spurs your passions?

Lifescaping

Courage is hope that has said its prayers.

ANNE BADANES, AGE 41

There's a knock at your door. You put down this book, get up from your recliner, and answer it. A mysterious stranger in a black overcoat and a gray fedora with a little yellow feather in the band is standing there. He says, "Here, I want you to have this," and hands you a certified check for $1,000,000. The money is yours to spend as you see fit. The catch is, you have to spend it in the next twelve months.

What will you do with it?

Hmmm. Let's see. You could fritter it away on a fast car, a trip to Vegas, or an extravagant wardrobe. Or you could use it to further your aims. Maybe you build a new home in the country for your family because that's what you've been working toward all along. Or you get your teeth capped, take acting lessons, and move to Los Angeles because you've always wanted to be in the movies. Or you buy a grand piano and hire the best teacher you can find because you have a burning ambition to play Carnegie Hall.

If you have a lifescape, you'll know pretty much immediately what to do with your windfall. You use it to launch your dream—or move your dream a giant step closer to reality, because you launched it a while back.

A lifescape is a master plan—a vision of who, what, and where you want to be. With a lifescape, you're moving toward something. Without one, you're either running away or simply drifting.

Lifescaping is the process of setting your internal compass. It's the process of drawing up a life itinerary. Implicit in the process of lifescaping is having the courage to determine the direction you're going to take with the time you have left. Lifescaping is the logical next step after you've decided you're going to have some say on how your life turns out. It starts to happen after you've declared. "Enough! I'm not going to react to the world—I'm going to make the world react to me." A good lifescape gives you the courage and confidence that go along with having a sense of mission. A lifescape is a game plan, a vision, a road map, a statement of intent.

But whatever you call it, coming up with one is no small feat. Creating a lifescape requires making tough choices. It means focusing more time and effort in one direction to the exclusion of others. It runs against human nature to trade off choices because, one, we're inherently greedy and, two, we live in an instant society. We insist on having whatever it is that we want immediately. This is not how life works. Life insists on patience and perseverance. Granted, you should maintain a balance between your various life journeys, but you can't follow all your paths with equal intensity.

A lifescape should describe a path to an overall goal with a series of smaller goals. Think of these smaller goals as stepping stones. Some you'll reach, others you'll miss. In order to minimize opportunities for failure, you may be tempted to avoid being too specific, too aggressive or too ambitious with your goals. Don't.

You have to make real choices. If your lifescape is devoid of any and all risk of failure, throw it out and start over again. Because you're probably not aiming high enough.

A lifescape also should include a timetable and a means to gauge your progress. Unless you set specific, measurable goals, both in terms of results and timing, you'll never know if you're moving toward your overall goal or away from it.

A lifescape also should address what risks you're willing to take. It should include a specific list of what things you're willing to sacrifice, surrender, or concede in order to achieve your overall goal.

The very act of putting down on paper what you want to accomplish over the next few months, years, or decades gives you control over your direction. The day-to-day drone of living can so overwhelm us that we lose sight of where we're headed. Suddenly, ten or twenty years go by, and you're in deep psychoanalysis because you've realized you're nowhere near where you want to be.

When you have a clear lifescape, you'll always be making progress, even when it might not seem like it. Living is seldom like riding along in a motorboat, where you can simply cruise in a straight line from Point A to Point B. Living is more like riding along in a sailboat, where you're subjected to the whimsy of the winds. In a sailboat, you have to tack from Point A to another point entirely, zigging and zagging back and forth from one point to another until, finally, you arrive at Point B. To everyone else, you may appear to be moving away from your destination. But sometimes, you have to take two steps backward to move a step forward.

Life is rarely a matter of simple linear patterns. More often, you have to contend with the forces of nature to get where you're going.

*   *   *

From the day I graduated from college, I've had some sort of written plan. The plans have often changed. That's okay. The key is that, in nearly every case, I made a conscious decision to change them instead of letting fate have its way.

When I began Richard Saunders International, I sharpened my focus on lifescaping considerably. Every three months, I would meet with a team of advisors, including my banker, lawyer, and accountant. I'd present a written plan for the coming quarter and a review of the previous quarter. Once a year, I'd lay out a longer term vision for the company.

The process—along with the comments I gathered at these meetings—are a large part of the reason the company is successful. When a new business is just getting started, you have a hypothesis about what it will be about—but it's only a theory. As a business progresses through the early going, it's liable to change direction dozens of times. Mine did. But by pausing every three months to look at where we'd been and where we were going, I was better able to lead the business instead of letting the forces at work in the marketplace pull and push it this way and that.

Now that my company is more established, I write a new plan only once a year. But I spend as much time crafting it, if not more. If your lifescape is done properly and you stick with it, while maintaining enough flexibility to leave room for contingencies, it gives direction to everything you do. It guides your priorities and helps you focus your attention and resources. It increases the likelihood that you'll be able to use your time, energy, and talent with optimal efficiency.

The form your plan takes is up to you. But you should have one, two, or three simple goals at the heart of it, each with its own specific deadline. Whatever else you want to include is restricted only by the bounds of your energy and imagination. But do yourself a favor: push it.

My preference when setting out on a task is to set an immedi-ate goal with a short deadline, something I can get to in a hurry. It helps me generate momentum quickly and gives me a chance to bask in the warm glow of accomplishment I get when I hit the tar-get. As time passes, I layer in more goals with both short- and long-term horizons.

List your preliminary goals. Lay them out like stepping stones to your larger goal. Keep them small and close together, so that the distance from one to the next doesn't exceed your stride. And keep them simple and personal. Make them relevant to you and you alone. Exactly what is it that YOU are going to do?

Let's say you're thinking about building a new home. Your first goal is not simply "Build a new home." It should be more along the lines of, "Save enough money from my paycheck to put a down payment on a piece of land." Be as specific as you can. List specific measures you intend to take to accomplish your prelimi-nary goals—as in "Spend less money on lunch," "Get a part-time job for six months," "Sell the nuclear warheads that have been cluttering my closet because I'll never use them."

The more specific you can be in terms of articulating your mis-sion and the steps needed to carry it out, the more likely you are to succeed. But make sure that what you're dreaming of is really what you want. Because the mere act of putting a goal down on paper has a way of making it real.

Think hard about what your dream is worth. What risks are you willing to take? What sacrifices are you willing to make? And remember that cost of achieving always turns out to be greater than you thought it would be when you were standing at the start-ing line.

Then again, that's part of the reason the exhilaration is so in-tense once you get there.

One Bite at a Time

It's a lot easier to find courage if you're moving.

MIKI REILLY, AGE 27

Y ou have a vision. Your lifescape is in place, and you're ready to take action. That means you're also poised to deal with your worst fears—those coarse, scaly monsters that life heaves at you from out of nowhere. Elsewhere in this book, we've called them "fear dragons."

If you let them, they'll keep you from taking even the most tentative first step. They'll surround you and pump your head full of excuses and reasons to do nothing. You have to defeat them, or they'll defeat you.

The most effective way to do battle with your greatest fears—and to make progress on your lifescape—is to divide them into pieces. Instead of grappling with the monster, dismember it limb by limb. Defeat it a piece at a time.

In 1728, Benjamin Franklin developed a system for life improvement. He defined it as "a bold and arduous project of arriving at moral perfection. I wished to live without committing any fault at any time."

Franklin divided his task into thirteen components:

TEMPERANCE: Eat not to dullness; drink not to elevation.

SILENCE: Speak not but what may benefit others or yourself; avoid trifling conversations.

ORDER: Let all your things have their places; let each part of your business have its time.

RESOLUTION: Resolve to perform what you ought; perform without fail what you resolve.

FRUGALITY: Make no expense but to do good to others or yourself, i.e. waste nothing.

INDUSTRY: Lose no time; be always employed in something useful; cut off all unnecessary actions.

SINCERITY: Use no hurtful deceit; think innocently and justly; and, if you speak, speak accordingly.

JUSTICE: Wrong none by doing injuries, or omitting the benefits that are your duty.

MODERATION: Avoid extremes; forbear resenting injuries so much as you think they deserve.

CLEANLINESS: Tolerate no uncleanliness in body, clothes, or habitation.

TRANQUILLITY: Be not disturbed at trifles, or at accidents common or unavoidable.

CHASTITY: Rarely use sexual intercourse but for health or offspring, never to dullness, weakness, or the injury of your own or another's peace or reputation.

HUMILITY: Imitate Jesus and Socrates.

The plan was designed to improve one part of Franklin's life at a time, attacking only a portion of the problem in any given week. Franklin put it this way:

> I judged it would be well not to distract my attention by attempting the whole at once, but to fix it on one of them at a time. Like him who, having a garden to weed, does not attempt to eradicate all the bad herbs at once, which would exceed his reach and his strength, but works on one of the beds at a time, and, having accomplished the first, proceeds to a second.

Franklin kept a notebook with a spreadsheet set aside for each week. Each page listed his virtues down the left side of the page, the days of the week across the top. He concentrated on one virtue each week while tracking his performance against the others each day.

> Thus, in the first week, my great guard was to avoid every least offense against Temperance, leaving the other virtues to their ordinary chance, only marking every evening the faults of the day.

His mission was not to achieve perfection in all areas, but to gather feedback and quantify his performance.

Franklin's sheet was handwritten. Today, the format would make an excellent computer spreadsheet. He listed the theme for the week at the top, and he marked failures for each virtue for that day with an X. There was a new sheet for each week. A sample sheet looked like this:

FOCUS FOR THIS WEEK: TEMPERANCE
Eat not to dullness; drink not to elevation

WEEK		SUN	MON	TUES	WED	THURS	FRI	SAT
1.	Temperance:	X	XXX	X	X		X	
2.	Silence:	X	X		X		X	
3.	Order:	XX	X	X	X	X	X	
4.	Resolution:			X				
5.	Frugality:		X					
6.	Industry:					X		
7.	Sincerity:	X	X		X		X	X
8.	Justice:			X		X		X
9.	Moderation:	X		X	X			
10.	Cleanliness:	X		X		X	X	
11.	Tranquillity:			X				
12.	Chastity:	X	XXX	X	X	X	X	X
13.	Humility:							

Proceeding through his list of thirteen virtues one per week, Franklin went through a complete course of life improvement in thirteen weeks. In a year, he could complete the course four times. And he could track his progress the whole time.

*   *   *

Franklin's system can be used today to help generate courage for facing larger-than-life challenges. It's a way for you to keep a tight grip on your lifescape mission—and a format for attacking your fear one small piece at a time. Instead of Franklin's virtues, you might list a series of personal goals. Or you might list the components of the tasks you'll need to complete in order to achieve your higher goal.

Let's say it's New Year's Eve. Around the world, more people are getting ready to delude themselves with more lies than on any other night of the year. Many are getting ready to resolve to lose weight. Maybe you're making the same resolution. Again. But this time, you mean it.

It takes courage to lose weight, because losing weight requires that you believe in yourself and that you have the self-confidence and ability to persevere. All sorts of fears, stresses, uncertainties, and anxieties are vying for your attention, working to wear down your courage, and blur your concentration.

So you sit down with your resolve and Franklin's systems. Here's how you might make it apply to you.

STEP ONE: Break the challenge into pieces you can deal with one at a time. List the following pieces:
- Exercise for thirty minutes a day
- Eliminate fried foods
- Eliminate sweets
- Participate in active, energetic activities with your children
- Reduce portion sizes (one Big Mac instead of two)

Your list should include all the major hurdles to leading a healthy lifestyle. You might zero in on a specific meal:

breakfast, lunch, or dinner. Or you might turn your attention to a specific eating challenge: too much fast food, too much ice cream, or too many snacks.

STEP TWO: Set up a schedule that lets you focus on achieving one goal per week.

STEP THREE: Track your progress. When you slip up, put an X in the appropriate spot.

Be honest. Stay with it.

Pretty soon, they'll be calling you Slim.

I was overwhelmed with challenges when I founded Richard Saunders International. Reading articles about other new businesses wasn't much help—nine out of ten new businesses go belly up.

In the early going, my business was like a dike that had sprouted more leaks than I could count. At first, I ran from one leak to another. Pretty soon, I ran out of fingers. Still, the hemorrhaging continued. I decided to take a different tack, isolating the worst leaks and concentrating on those one at a time; focusing on issues that, in and of themselves, could put me out of business. I thought of them as Business Death Threats.

The first issue was to increase sales. The second was to collect money and manage cash flow. The third was to improve our services. I didn't forget about all the other leaks—I simply dedicated extra time and resources to one Death Threat at a time, until it had been brought under control and I could move on to the next. I kept this up for two years until the company had arrived at a point where it was no longer necessary for me to stay up late at night, bathed in cold sweat.

Think about your circumstances. What are the components

of your fear? How can you break your Death Threats into bite-size pieces? Where are the weak spots in your challenge? What part of your problem can you attack first and, early in the process, generate courage and confidence for the rest of your journey?

Use Journal Writing to Expose Your Mind

Courage is to say what you believe in your heart, without fearing the consequences.

DIANE ISEMAN

When you allow fear to incubate in the dark corners of your imagination, it can loom larger than life. There, it can sink roots, drain your will and leave you paralyzed. In the realm of imagination, fear can take over, until the distinction between reality and your fears is lost. But take heart—you can defeat your fears in the pages of a journal.

Keeping a journal gives you an advantage over your fear. It forces fear out into the open where you can get a good look at it. In the pages of a journal, you can examine your fear to determine just how large or how small it really is. You can study it from this angle and that, trace it to its source and find out what gives it strength. You can dissect your fear into small pieces, which you can attack one at a time.

With a journal, you can give your fear a name. And naming it will give you power over it. On paper or on the screen of a word processor, you can do to your fear what your fear has been doing to you. In the process, you'll begin to realize that the fear is your fear—in its precise form, it belongs to no one but you. And because it's your fear, it's yours to command, diminish, and ultimately banish—if only you take authority over it. Once you see your fear for what it is and understand the power you have over it, you'll have removed the obstacles between yourself and courage.

In the pages of your journal, you can reconsider and redefine yourself. You can separate your fantasies from your dreams. And you can chart a path for your future.

Putting your thoughts, observations, fears, dreams, and emotions into a written form, even if only on a semi-regular basis, is a way to measure your progress on each of our life journeys. It's also a way to make progress; by giving voice to your dreams, you make them more familiar and, in so doing, more accessible.

You may prefer to keep a journal in your computer. Computer journals have the advantage of making it easy to password-protect them from prying eyes; the more "secure" your journal, the more likely you are to be candid with your feelings.

You can turn to your journal whenever the need arises. Sometimes, I find myself adding to my journal a couple times in a week. Then there are times when a month or two goes by between entries. Either way, it's there for me when I feel the need to return to it.

The feeling of discovery and liberation I get from reading entries I made a month, six months, or three years ago is empowering. Often, a huge, hulking fear from the past becomes barely a footnote in the present, usually because I've been able to defeat it or because time and events have eroded it away.

I got into the habit of keeping a journal in a roundabout way. My grandmother made a deal with each of her grandchildren when we went off to college. If we would write her a letter each week telling her what we were up to, she promised she'd write back. To sweeten the deal, she'd put a five dollar bill in the envelope.

I profited far more from sitting down each week to write those letters than I did from my grandmother's bribe. The process smoothed out my college years by imposing a sense of sequence to them. It helped each week flow from and build on the previous week. Themes developed as I explored possibilities and explored different career prospects with my grandmother through the U.S. Postal Service. And it forced me to put my thoughts down on paper, thus confronting my fear of writing.

Don't worry about what to write in your journal. Don't let the blank pages intimidate you. Write whatever comes to mind. Listen to your heart and empty your feelings onto the pages. And remember that a life worth living is a life worth writing about.

Think about it. What has happened when you've given your fears free rein in your imagination? How could you begin to articulate your fears in writing? How could you gain control over them by putting them down on paper?

Brian Conlan was a seventeen-year-old boy who kept a journal. In its pages, he named fears that would cripple most people. In his words, he discovered and defined himself.

He'd known for two years that he had cancer. The doctors called it osteogenic sarcoma. In his journal, Brian called it "this stranger in my body."

After all the chemotherapy and seven major surgeries, Brian finally ran out of medical options. He wasn't afraid of dying. He was afraid only of what he would miss by no longer being alive. And in the dark moments, he would find courage in his poetry.

When he learned about his condition, for example, he wrote a poem. He called it "The Shadow." In his verse, he faced his fear head on. And he showed it no mercy:

> *Everything in life was great,*
> *all was well,*
> *and nothing in the world*
> *could stop me now.*
> *It would be a new year,*
> *a fresh start*
> *from a bumpy past in this place.*
> *All in life was great,*
> *and then the lights went out,*
> *the sun went down,*
> *and it cast a shadow on my future.*
> *It was all of a sudden, so unexpected,*
> *sitting with this horrid shadow.*
> *All in life was great,*
> *though others hated darkness*
> *and cried with their shadow,*
> *I became used to*
> *this stranger in my body.*
> *In and out I went*
> *from the shadow's yard,*
> *his favorite place,*
> *where we all have darkness . . .*
> *This evil darkness that creeps around*
> *bugs me sometimes,*
> *but not always.*
> *And as I know the shadow's hard,*
> *I cannot forget*
> *All in life is great.*

Brian filled his journal with his poetry. It helped him pack a lifetime into the final two years of his life. And when his time came, he drifted off quietly, gracefully, unafraid. He died at home, in his father's arms, which is how he'd wanted it to be. Somewhere in the reaches of his semiconsciousness as he lay in the bed, he heard his father, John, tell him once more that he loved him. Brian had just enough breath left to answer. "Love you," he said. Then he was gone.

Brian had decided it didn't make sense to complain. Instead, he wrote poetry. His journal enabled him to drag his fears out into the open, and he became stronger for it. The cancer took his life, but it failed to break his spirit. It wasn't so much that he defied his condition. It wasn't so much, as the phrase so often goes, that he "battled cancer." It was more that he lived his life. He galloped after it eagerly, valiantly.

And he filled the blank pages of his journal with the tracks of a hero.

Tony Anderson kept a journal, too—but for a reason different than Brian's. Instead of writing to deal with his fears, Tony wrote to escape the cruel confines of his body.

Tony's tired body gave out a few days before Christmas. The consensus was that he'd had a massive heart attack. Complicated by pneumonia. Complicated by diabetes. He was forty-nine years old, and his trial had begun twenty years earlier. He woke up one morning with a stiffness in his neck. It wasn't long before he was unable to hold a fork in his left hand without dropping it.

A specialist told him it was amyotrophic lateral sclerosis, also known as ALS, also known as Lou Gehrig's disease. The specialist explained that it destroys the nerves that control muscle movement. One year after waking up with a stiff neck, Tony was an in-valid.

The doctors gave him three years. Sooner or later, they said, something would get him. Pneumonia, probably. Tony fooled them. But for most of the past two decades, he was a captive of his ruined body. He was fed through a hole in his stomach. One machine kept him breathing; another sucked fluid from his lungs. The only muscles he could still control were the ones around his eyes and his mouth. While he could no longer speak, he found ways to express himself. A blink of his eyes meant yes; clenching his jaw muscles meant no.

But his spirit was good. So was his memory. He was into the fifth chapter of his journal when the end came.

He was storing his life in a computer. A sensor attached to a band around his head picked up signals triggered by a twitch of his eyebrow. The impulse traveled through the wire to the screen at the edge of the bed, selected a letter from the alphabet, and added it to his slowly developing sequence of thoughts. It was a tedious process—one letter at a time, then a word, then a sentence. A paragraph no longer than this might take an hour. But his writing carried him away from the nursing home. It gave him legs, put strength back in his arms. It may well have kept him from giving up. In his mind, he could watch long ago skies turn orange and purple at sunset. He could smell the coffee brewing over campfires on family outings. Or feel his bare feet dangling in the Ohio River. Or experience once again the sudden tug of a bass on his line.

Tony let David Wecker read the first three chapters of his journal a few months before he died. He hoped to have his journal completed in a couple years. His only real fear was that he wouldn't live long enough to finish it. "Toward the end, I didn't know how to pray," his mother, Rita Burke, told David. "I didn't forget exactly. But I didn't know whether to ask God to take him to end his pain or to leave him here so he could finish his writing. Because I knew how important it was to him."

When Tony died, Rita said, she went to pieces. "I never cried in front of Tony, because then he'd cry, too. But this time, I went to pieces. Then I went inside. It sounds crazy, but he had a glow. He wasn't smiling, but there was like a shining around him. A peacefulness. The nurse noticed it, too."

Tony used his journal to take himself away from a situation that, without it, would have been hopeless. It didn't matter so much that he didn't finish it. It mattered more that he found a way, through his writing, to hold on to his life—and to make it mean something.

Putting your thoughts on paper can help you through all sorts of circumstances—including everyday hassles that fall far short of debilitating diseases. The process has a way of driving away all kinds of fear dragons. Our minds allow us to perpetuate fuzzy thinking. On paper, thoughts are forced to become more distinct, more rational, easier to consider.

Put this book down for a moment, grab a pencil and a sheet of paper and write down whatever you're thinking. Simply shake out the thoughts swirling inside your head onto the paper. Continue writing until all your core thoughts, fears and feelings have been translated into written words.

The result is a sort of mental EKG. Study it closely, doctor. What's really on your mind? How long have these thoughts been floating around in your head? How can you resolve some of the issues and get rid of them? What is the ratio of positive to negative thoughts in your mind?

Is it the mindset of someone on the brink of an adventure or the verge of a victory?

Maybe you can't control much of what's going on around you. But if you take pen in hand, you can control your thoughts and where they take you.

To Thine Own Self
Be True

Courage is heeding your own advice, rather than the advice of others.

NICOLE UTTAMA SHARMA, AGE 17

B e true to yourself. You'll never be sorry.

I'm not talking about being true to yourself in the sense of grabbing all you can get or setting yourself up as a number one. I'm talking about being true to yourself in terms of knowing what's the right thing to do for yourself and then doing it—taking tangible steps to make your dream happen, writing the expectations of others out of your life equation, and persevering against adversity.

Have the courage of your convictions. This assumes you have convictions. Without a strong code of values, you might as well be wading in quicksand. When you have a fundamental set of beliefs, you have a solid basis for courage. Once you have that spiritual foundation, you can head out in any direction you choose, knowing you have everything you need to face the challenges you come up against. Because at that point, you will be sufficient in and of yourself. You'll have conviction; therefore, you'll have courage. Most of all, be honest with yourself and the fears you encounter along the way. The person you hurt most by not being honest with yourself is . . . you guessed it.

My brother, Bruce, is not afraid to speak his mind. He has a healthy disrespect for authority and convention. He also spent time at Procter & Gamble—where, at one point, he was assigned to work on a marketing program for Metamucil aimed mainly at physicians.

Bruce surveyed the situation and decided what Metamucil needed was a mascot—a Speedy Alka-Seltzer, a Reddy Kilowatt, or a Pillsbury Doughboy to call its own. It was a groundbreaking plan, inasmuch as no laxative had ever had a mascot. The conventional take on laxatives is, they're not supposed to be fun. They're supposed to be serious medicine. The pressure to keep Metamucil respectable, in the conventional sense, was intense. But Bruce wanted to drag it out of the closet—or at least, the medicine chest. And he wasn't afraid to articulate his thoughts, in his own way.

That's how Mr. Happy Bowel came into being. Mr. Happy Bowel was an intestinal version of Mr. Peanut, but with more of a song-and-dance attitude. Bruce had two T-shirts designed for key Metamucil distributors and customers—one with the slogan, "Mr. Happy Bowel Is Moving Out," and the other, "With Friends Like These, Who Needs Enemas?"

Mr. Happy Bowel shocked a lot of people at Metamucil. But in the medical marketing world, he became a phenomenon. Years later, Bruce still was getting calls from physicians and P&G'ers hoping to glom on to one of those T-shirts.

My entrepreneurial vision has succeeded largely because it was my own. It was what was right for me. Other dreams are more outlandish and, consequently, more fear-filled. Ken Davis's dream is an example. It wasn't the sort of dream that inspired the confidence of those closest to him. It was an odd, quirky kind of dream.

But Ken's story is a classic example of the power of following your dream—and of being who you really are. In my opinion, Ken has the sort of courage, tenacity, and vision it took to make this country what it is today.

My wife and I are two of Ken's satisfied customers. He offers a hard-to-find service that, sooner or later, just about everyone could use. It's a service that makes a lot of sense. Still, I would've loved to have been a fly on the wall when Ken told his wife, Jane, he'd decided what he wanted to do with the rest of his life. Ken says she laughed at first.

"Looking back, I don't blame her," said Ken, who is the thirty-nine-year-old founder, president, and CEO of Cincinnati Doorbell and Chimes, a company of one. "Most people can't believe a person can make a living fixing doorbells. In fact, the number-one question I'm asked is, 'How can you make a living fixing doorbells?'"

The way Ken remembered it, Jane laughed out loud for a whole minute. Then she saw Ken wasn't laughing—at which point, she began to cry.

The truth about Ken is, he wasn't cut out to work for someone else. For five years, he was a sales rep for R. J. Reynolds Tobacco, in charge of the fifth-largest territory for generic cigarettes in America. One of his responsibilities was to go around to all his customers and, wherever his generic cigarettes were displayed, dust the display with a feather duster. "It struck me as silly," Ken said. "The company didn't like me, and I didn't like the company."

So he went to work for his brother-in-law, who owns a company that sells doors. Whenever he called on a customer, he noticed that, half the time, the customer's doorbell was on the fritz. "There'd be this little sign taped over the bell that said, DOORBELL DOESN'T WORK—PLEASE KNOCK," he said. "I found that, with nearly two out of five doors I knocked on, the doorbell didn't work."

Whenever he found a malfunctioning doorbell, he'd ask in a subtle way why the doorbell's owner had never had it repaired. "Two reasons," he said. "One, people don't know who to call. They've never heard of a doorbell repairman. Two, they figure it's going to cost them a second mortgage. So they let it slide."

At the time, the bell at Ken's front door was on the blink. So he called a few electricians and asked what it would take to fix it. "They all told me it was gonna cost $82 plus the service call," Ken said. "In other words, they didn't want to mess with it." Then he called the Cincinnati building inspector's office and asked if there was any law requiring one to be an electrician to fix doorbells for a living. "The guy laughed and said, 'No, because if all you're doing is doorbells—and buzzers and chimes—you're dealing with low-voltage electricity.'"

It was about that time that Ken told Jane what he wanted to do with the rest of his life. The next day, he bought a $9 doorbell kit at the hardware store. He took it home and experimented with it, learning all he could about the four components of any doorbell system—your button, your transformer, your wire, your bell.

Ken came by my house one day to repair my doorbell. At that time, he figured it would take him four months to get caught up on all the jobs he landed as a result of his booth at the Cincinnati Home and Garden Show a few weeks earlier.

The thing is, Ken had found his niche. He'd been true to his vision, no matter how odd or quirky it seemed to everybody else. And as far as he knew, he was the only full-time doorbell repairman in a world filled with doorbells. "I'm a happy guy," he said. "No more kicking the dog when I get home at night."

Embarking on a career as a doorbell repairman is no small challenge—especially when you have a wife, a son, and a dog to support like Ken did. It requires an investment of courage. But once Ken made the investment, he began reaping benefits that were natural consequences of living the dream that was right for him.

All along, he'd had the freedom to pursue him dream. That much was guaranteed to him under the U.S. Constitution. But it wasn't until he actually exercised that freedom—until he was true to himself—that he became a free man. Because once he was true to himself, all the pieces began falling into place.

Think about your dreams. When you're lying in bed at night, thinking about getting up and going to work tomorrow, think: where would you rather be? If you do nothing to change your circumstances, how do you imagine you will spend the rest of your life?

When you were younger, what did you want to be? What kept that from happening?

Why not now?

You Must Continue the Journey from Where You Are

Live each day like it's your last and eventually you'll be right.

URBAN CARMICHAEL

I lost track of the time . . ."

"If it weren't for this bum leg . . ."

"Honey, I have a perfectly reasonable explanation . . ."

"The dog ate my homework . . ."

Stop making excuses!

The buck stops with you. You are the Chosen One, the leader of your life. It's up to you, O Great One, to blaze the trail as you head into the wilderness. You alone are responsible for the success of your life.

As such, you have to continue your life journey from where you are at this moment. Please, no whining! You can't move forward when you're whining. You have to dance with the person you accompanied to the prom. Unless you've found a way to go back in time and rearrange the past, you don't have an option—you have to proceed with your lifescape from your current position. Yesterday is too late. The only tenses in which you can have impact are the present and the future.

Learn from the past, don't fret over it. Live today and face toward the future. As you approach tomorrow, don't let feelings of injustice hold you back. In our society, we're all too ready to blame lost opportunities on some form of prejudice against age, race, or sexual orientation. Replaying in your mind the many ways in which you've been wronged does nothing to make tomorrow better. The only one who suffers when you refuse to let old wounds heal is yourself.

Unless you know the exact date and time your death is scheduled to take place, you're never too old to try something new or change something old. As long as you live, there's always going to be someone telling you you're either too young or too old. Either way, once you start believing it, the age issue is nothing more than an excuse for doing nothing.

The only problem with long-term procrastination is that, sometimes, it becomes progressively more difficult to pull ourselves up out of ruts. This is partly because we tend to define ourselves in terms of the work we do. We tie our egos and sense of self-esteem to our careers. And the corporate world reinforces the process. As our career journeys continue, we become comfortable in our supposed fields of expertise and spend less time exploring new skills. We become addicted to our bonuses, our company cars and our regular paychecks—to the point where we lose ourselves. We forget that, once upon a time, we got along quite nicely without perks.

How does it happen? When we embark on our careers, we're filled with a sense of adventure and a passion for learning, discovering, and making a mark. As we enter middle age, we become more concerned with defending our positions and looking over our shoulders, because we're worried someone might be gaining on us. Our energy is funneled through a defensive mentality that results in an unwillingness to take risks, making it nearly impossible to leave our corporate cocoons and start our own businesses, even when that's what we want to do.

It's sad when people in corporate settings keep their noses to the grindstone and their eyes on their wallets, only to discover they've gone the wrong direction. Imagine how you'd feel one day to look up and realize you're way off course. Imagine being locked into a life with no connection to your true passion. But the money is too good, and you're afraid to change.

Think about it. You can change whenever you decide to change. Yesterday doesn't matter. There's still time to shape tomorrow, if you start today.

That's what Frank Petrello did. After seventy-five years of yesterdays, he decided he'd put off his dream long enough. It didn't matter that, by conventional standards, he no longer had the looks or the body. All that mattered was the dream. And the time had come for him to get on with it.

I read about Frank in David Wecker's column in the *Cincinnati Post*. Frank is a dancer with the Hot Knights Male Revue out of Cleveland. The Hot Knights performed mostly at nightclubs and the occasional bachelorette or birthday party. Frank was the only Hot Knight eligible for Social Security. They call him "Disco Frankie, the Dancing Machine."

"Frankie looks like what you think a seventy-five-year-old guy would look like," said Hot Knight Damien Milicevic, who was forty-five years younger than Frank. "He is an average seventy-five-year-old man with a lot of lead in his pencil, put it that way."

Frank got into the music. Usually, he would come onstage in his caveman costume, the one with the cape. He had other routines, too—Santa Claus, Cupid, Jason with the hockey mask, a pizza delivery boy. None of this rankled Frank's wife in the least.

As far as Carmella Petrello was concerned, if her man was having a good time, it was okay with her. She was sixteen when she married Frank. That was fifty-six years ago. By the time he started dancing with the Hot Knights, she was bedridden with arthritis. But Frankie took good care of her.

"He always worked real hard," Carmella said. "He always liked dancing, too. But he was all the time working at the GM plant and selling real estate because he had a family. Five boys and one girl. And now, eighteen grandchildren. So when he got older, we let him go. We let him do what he wanted to do. He was entitled."

Eight years earlier, Frank decided to let what was inside him come out. He became Disco Frankie. A few years went by and someone decided he had to be the oldest male stripper in the world. He appeared on *Donahue* and *Jenny Jones*. Those were the only times Carmella ever saw her husband perform in public. She remembered lying there in bed, not thinking anything about it, that it was wrong or anything, just laughing until tears flowed from her eyes. "Frankie's dancing don't bother me at all," she said. "He's proud of what he does. The kids are proud of him, too. They think it's terrific for his age and all. And he never gives me anything to worry about. Frankie's a good man."

He'd fulfilled his obligations to his family. The time had come for him to fulfill his obligation to himself. Granted, his vision for himself is wildly eccentric. Imagine how his friends might have responded when he told them what he had in mind. Imagine how you might have responded if he were your father.

It would have been easy for Frank to let his age or what other people thought discourage him. It would have been easier to take up bingo or shuffleboard. Instead, he chose to be loyal to his dream.

*   *   *

Everyone has strengths. Everyone has weaknesses. We're obligated to do as much as we can with what we're given. Robert Mister was given less than most, but he has the gumption and the will to do more than most people who have far more in the way of education, earning power, and natural ability than he does. Robert is the best example I know for why it's so important to continue the journey from where you are.

Robert is a slow learner. He doesn't mind telling you. His formal education consists of two and a half years of elementary school. He remembered going to school one day and having his teacher tell him he might as well not come back the next. So he didn't.

That was before he learned to read or write. But the remarkable thing about Robert was, while it takes him longer than most people to learn something, once he gets a piece of learning in his head, it stays there. "And you cannot beat me on money," he says. "I got a calculator and a sales-tax card I take with me when I go to a store, so I always know what I'm supposed to pay and how much change I'm supposed to get back."

Robert is fifty-three years old. He wears a shirt with his name embroidered on it. Mister Robert Mister. And he makes his living washing windows. He has sixty-some clients in all, mostly businesses around the campus of the University of Cincinnati.

For thirty-two years, he has been doing windows. Before that, he had a job at a coin-operated laundry, keeping the place tidy. "They had some fella who did their windows. Half the time, he'd show up and half the time he wouldn't. So the man I worked for at the laundry said, 'I'll give you $5 extra a week to do my windows.' That's when I got it in my head, 'Hey, there's plenty of places that have windows that need cleaning. I could do windows all the time.' It was my own idea."

There's a stigma to washing windows. A lot of people, if you ask them, will say, "I don't do windows," no matter how dirty they are. But Robert finds something satisfying in starting out with a dirty window and ending up with a clean one. He also appreciates the fact that he doesn't have a boss telling him when he can call it a day.

"I make my own honest living, and I have a way to show people my dependability," he says. "I got my own house, too. A two-family on Martin Luther King Drive. Paid twenty-eight thousand cash for it. And I paid fifteen thousand cash to get it remodeled. New windows, new sink, stuff like that. All paid for."

No one would blame Robert if he decided to stop paying Social Security and began instead to collect it. It certainly would make his life easier, and he certainly would qualify for benefits. But that isn't his way; that isn't much of a way to show his dependability.

"I'm lucky to be born with what I was born with," he says. "You see a lot of people, they don't have this, they don't have that. So what do they do? They feel sorry for themselves.

"God don't like that ignorant stuff. God wants you to take what you have and do something good with it."

Well said, Robert.

Think about your dream. And realize it can't begin to happen until you find the courage to take the first step, even if it's only a small step. Stop saving yourself for tomorrow. Start living now.

You have the ability to control your life. You have the heart, the courage and the brains to enrich your life journey. So what are you waiting for? You are where you are. Start from there. Start now.

Your dream will come true only if you have the courage to be true to yourself. Cling to the words of Ben Franklin:

Up sluggard and waste not life, in the grave will be sleeping enough.

Take heart. Be brave. And may God bless you.

We Want to Hear from You!

Thanks for letting David and me into your life for this short time. We'd like to know what you think about *Making the Courage Connection*—which chapters you liked, which you didn't, and what effect, if any, this book has had on your life.

Please send us a picture postcard. We love picture postcards. We issued a similar invitation with our last book—and we sent a handwritten response to each postcard we received that had a legible return address. We'd like to do the same thing with this book. But please be patient; we've learned that postcards come in floods and, because we answer them personally, it might take a few months for us to respond to them properly.

Send picture postcards to:

Making the Courage Connection
Richard Saunders International
3851 Edwards Road
Cincinnati, Ohio 45244

Please print your return address at the top of your card—the U.S. Postal Service's zip code stickers cover the bottoms of post-cards.

Or if you prefer, you can send an E-mail to us directly at: EurekaM@aol.com. Sooner or later, we'll send one back.

To respond to two common requests in advance:

1. No, I will not hire you. I have the greatest staff in the world and absolutely no interest in adding to it.
2. No, I will not review your idea. If you send unsolicited ideas for new products or services, my lawyer has asked that I inform you herewith that they automatically become my property. Besides, you'll be much better off if you push your ideas forward on your own, using your newfound courage.

Richard Saunders International offers two services:

1. *Eureka! Brainstorming:* A service focused on inspiring true new-to-the-world ideas.
2. *InterACT Inventing:* A service focused on translating seed idea inspirations into integrated, practical business solutions.
3. *Eureka! Institute Training:* Interactive lecture programs on innovation, creativity, and courage.

To learn more:
    Call (513) 271-9911 or
    Fax (513) 271-9966 or
    E-mail EurekaM@aol.com

About the Authors

DOUG HALL is the founder and CEO of Richard Saunders International, a think tank of strategic inventors whose mission is "to inspire breakthrough ideas and nurture the courage to take action on them." Doug and his team of Trained Brains® at the Eureka! Ranch provide wisdom and inspiration for executives at such organizations as Nike, Walt Disney, Kellogg's, Procter & Gamble, AT&T, American Express, Minnesota Power, and even the United States Congress.

Doug's passion for adventure extends to his diverse hobbies: the bagpipes, juggling, magic, scuba diving, photography, genealogy, vintage port, and English lordships. Doug is the rightful Lord of Threshfield, thanks to a winning bid at a London auction. He is married to his high school sweetheart, Debbie, and has three children, Kristyn, Tori, and Brad.

DAVID WECKER is a Richard Saunders International Trained Brain. He writes a column for the *Cincinnati Post* and cohosts a call-in talk show on WLW radio. David is a musician and beekeeper, the Lord of Kirkby on the Moor, and the father of two children, Sam and Betsy.